Unequivocal Love

Unequivocal Love

My Spiritual Journey

ROLAND R. J. ROBERT

Library and Archives Canada Cataloguing in Publication

Robert, Roland R. J., 1949-, author
  Unequivocal love / Roland R.J. Robert.

ISBN 978-0-9958920-0-2 (softcover)
ISBN 978-0-9958920-1-9 (e-book)

1. Robert, Roland R. J., 1949-. 2. Spirituality. 3. Spiritual
life. I. Title.

BL73.R63A3 2017 204.092 C2017-900993-1

Book layout and design by The Review,
Vankleek Hill, Ontario.

Printed by lulu.com

March 2017.

Table of Contents

Introduction 1
Prayer. 3
Flight from Evil. 7
The Bible 15
Genesis. 19
Sin 25
Judgment. 31
Submission. 33
Hell. 35
Mary. 39
Joseph 43
Throwing Stones. 47
Wealth 53
Love 57
Faith. 61
Miracles 65
Me and Judas. 69
The Passion of Christ 71
Christ Crucified 75
Christianity 79
Religious Social Club 83
Idolatry. 85
Sex and Homosexuality. 87
What is Forgiveness? 89
Abortion 91
Body and Soul 93
Tranquility 97
Death 101

Introduction

God has graced me with work that involved a lot of time alone. For the most part, I've been a transport driver and have visited most of North America. Raised on religious beliefs, for a period of time I laid my convictions aside and lived a life that I thought was free. However, my belief in God was deeply seeded. Only when I went in search of him did I realize that while I thought I was free without God in my life, I was only lying to myself. The outer layer of my being was living in pleasure while the core was slowly rotting.

Thanks to some friends who will always be close to my heart and the charismatic movement of the eighties, I began to pray. Being told that I could ask God for signs of his existence – I did so, and to my astonishment, I received more than I had asked for. Did I get struck by lightning and wake up in the morning a changed man? Not in this lifetime. Instead, in his kindness and eternal patience he took me one step at a time, leaving me in the lifestyle I thought I wanted to live while quietly, like a whisper, encouraging me to follow a different path. Today I see that as he saw I was ready, he placed people and events on my route to guide me. If I didn't choose the direction he wanted for me, he didn't get angry or leave me alone, but patiently and lovingly continued to offer me other options. I now know that he will never close one door without opening another and will continue to do so for as long as I am on this earth.

I, for the greater part of my life, believed that God was a judge sitting on a throne somewhere in a space I didn't (and don't) understand, waiting for me to die so that with all of my sins he could send me to eternal damnation. I don't think I am the only one to have, or have had such feelings. So I decided to read the bible and listened to it on tape. I asked myself questions and asked questions of others. I spoke to religious people of different denominations and ordinary people of little religious study, and some who claimed to be non-believers. I spent many hours in my journeys meditating on the issues that disturbed me, and asking questions.

Now, as I write I discover there are more questions than answers in my quest for God. This book is not meant to preach but to present my discoveries so that you (the reader) may reach your own conclusions and ask your own questions. These chapters contain part of my journey and some of my thoughts – *which remain questions.*

Roland R. J. Robert

Prayer

(The Power and the Promise)

When I say that 30 years ago (January 1985) I lost my business, my family and my home all in one day and spent the first two weeks of February in a hospital, constantly crying and repeating that the next 20 years would not be like the last, some people might think this is another story of a bereaved person turning to God because he/she was weak and needed a crutch. I've read many wonderful testimonials where God gave someone strength in times of weakness or carried them in his arms when they needed a crutch, but such is not my story.

Although I knew of God's existence as a judge waiting to send me to hell for my many sins, I was an "on again, off again" Christian. I hadn't even thought of turning to him in my time of trouble. If anything, I held him responsible for my problems because my common-law spouse had begun searching for her faith and this caused friction between us.

It was God who came to me. Why, I don't know. I blame it on the prayers of my relatives and friends, especially my parents who never gave up on me. I owe it to the Blessed Virgin, Saint Anne *(whose shrine I'd visited two years before)* and mostly to Jesus, who died for my sins. God came to me because of the one thing I knew nothing about … Love.

It began on a Sunday morning in March when I received a phone call from my common-law wife, whom I had recently abandoned. After cheating on her, I thought she should hate me, but instead she put aside her pain and invited me to accompany her for a mini-conference at the local church that afternoon. Without hesitation, I agreed. I wasn't interested in church or the conference, but I did want to be with her. Perhaps I could entice her to go out for supper or something afterwards. Maybe I could re-ignite the spark.

God, however, seems to get a yes however he can and so I was off to church. At first I was bored and anxious to leave but the narrator had a way of catching one's attention. He never once spoke of hellfire or the book of judgment. Not once did he speak of repentance. Instead he spoke of God's love, the Blessed Virgin Mary and the Holy Rosary. He told a humorous story of a farmer who approached him after one of his sermons. Their conversation had gone like this:

"Father," the farmer said, "I understand what you're saying but I don't have time to say the Rosary. I get up at four in the morning to milk my cows and by the time I've completed all my chores at night, I'm just too tired to pray."

The narrator asked, "How many cows do you have, my friend?"

"I've got 50 milk cows," replied the farmer.

"Well," said the narrator, "One Hail Mary per cow you milk and you've said the Rosary."

By this time I was paying attention and almost forgot about the lady beside me. I couldn't believe what I was hearing. Growing up, I had to say the Rosary in church or with my parents from time to time. This was done while ceremoniously kneeling straight as a board. Sitting on my heels or leaning on an object was strictly taboo and I had to fold my hands and assume a solemn attitude of penitence. Now this priest was telling me I could pray anytime and anywhere. He spoke of the love and benefits of prayer as a means of communicating with a loving God. Wow! When he spoke of the 15 promises of the Rosary I had a lump in my throat.

After the conference, the narrator gave each of us a plastic Rosary. As I received mine, my legs became weak and I began to tremble. I felt empty, as if I were looking at a picture of a lost loved one. I hung it over the mirror of my car thinking that since it took me 30 minutes to drive to work at night, this might be a good time to try prayer.

At first, reciting the Rosary wasn't an easy task. I had to try to remember some of the prayers and I found that as I struggled through it I got very tired and sleepy. Sometimes I wondered if I would fall asleep at the wheel of my car, but I decided to keep praying and let God do the rest. Some nights I didn't want to pray and I had to force myself to go on.

Changes in my life didn't occur overnight as I continued to say the Rosary while still living the party lifestyle. It took over a year for me to finally give myself to God and ask him to come into my life as my savior, and it's only thereafter that my life took on a new meaning.

Somewhere along the line, I received pamphlets that taught me the rest of the prayers *(besides the Our Father and Hail Mary)*. I learned of the mysteries of the Rosary and discovered what a wonderful way to contemplate the life of Jesus they are. Reciting the Rosary with family or in a prayer group is a very special and profound spiritual experience. Yet, when I'm alone there's a one-on-one intimacy and I feel I'm sharing my day with God – perhaps in a more personal manner.

My search for my individual relationship with God has been an eventful journey that continues even after 30 years. Whether it was me saying it or God using my own voice so that I would hear it, the last 30 years haven't been the same. I still get wet when it rains and I don't see a halo when I look in the mirror but this I hold to be true; God has given me back my dignity. He continues to teach me to love myself, others and mostly him. He's bringing me to acceptance and fills me with a desire to seek him.

He has also given me three very special gifts. In 1999, I met a wonderful woman who has since become my loving wife and a true blessing in my life. In 2001, I was reunited with my son, whom I hadn't seen for over 25 five years. Then, in 2003, God gave me the strength to accept the passing of my beloved mother.*

NOTE: This was previously published in the Annals of St. Anne de Beaupré January-February 2007 issue Vol. 121 – No. 1, page 21.

Flight from Evil

Long grey hair, a beard and mustache, with a deep frown, and piercing angry eyes that would frighten even the most pious; his hair and robes flowing around him as if blown by a powerful wind. On a desk before him lay a thick open book below which was written the word 'Judgment'. This picture from an old catechism book haunted me throughout my youth and still returns to me some 50 years later. The teacher of my catechism class said we had to behave because God wrote everything we did in that book and one day he would judge us for our sins.

Jesus nailed to the cross with his eyes looking skyward, blood seeping from his hands and feet, as well as from his side and his crown of thorns.

"We did this," I was told.

"Jesus died for our sins and when we sin, we assist in his crucifixion." By the time I was 15, I knew I wouldn't be going to heaven because I had sinned too often. I was afraid of God and didn't want to look at the crucifix to see what I had done to Jesus. As much as I could, I stayed away from church and religion.

Still, a part of me remained fascinated by God, Jesus and the Virgin Mary. I remember one night when I was about six or seven years old, I had a dream where the Blessed Virgin appeared and told me to change my ways. The next morning I told my friend about my dream and we decided to change, but that only lasted for a few hours and then we were back to being normal kids and I don't recall dreaming of the Virgin Mary again.

My youth and adolescence was lived like any other. I thought of sports, and hanging out, and girls, and thought very little of God or the afterlife. When I became an adult I married, had a child and when I turned 25, I divorced my wife. One day I met another young woman, a single mother of three, and fell in love. I asked her out for our first date and she agreed, then she asked me to go to church with her on Sunday and I agreed as long as we sat near the back, since I had not attended mass in years and had forgotten what to do.

When I walked up the steps of the church with her that Sunday I noticed the cornerstone of the building was dated 1949. It impressed me that the church was built the year of my birth. We sat in the back as agreed and waited for the service to begin. I felt a hand on my shoulder and when I turned a gentleman asked if I would assist in passing the collection plate. Embarrassed, I informed him of my dilemma and he pointed to where he would be seated. He said to keep an eye on him and he would let me know when it was time. After the service, she and I laughed and I jokingly stated that God was getting back at me for missing church all those years. *(Now I wonder if he wasn't calling me.)*

The lady and I spent the next eight years together and raised her children, and for a while I thought I had it all. Then she became more and more interested in religion while I turned the other way. It's not that I didn't believe; I was convinced I was already doomed because of my sins, and was afraid to face Jesus.

In 1984 Pope Jean Paul II came to Ottawa. By then, we owned a restaurant and decided to close it for this special day. My wife wanted desperately to go see the Pope, to the point of crying and pleading with me, but I had a guy come over to do work on the roof of my business instead. I was sure I had it made. I was the big-shot businessman, with a common-law wife, and three wonderful children. Then, in January of 1985, my crystal chandelier came crashing down. In December of 1984 I had everything and by February of 1985 everything I had left was in the back of my old Volaré station wagon. My business was bankrupt and my wife and I had separated.

———

I stepped out of the elevator and stared at the bleak, cold, unwelcoming wall in front of me. I heard the voice of the burly male nurse telling me to turn right, and I walked toward the large swinging doors at the far end of the corridor. I felt like his voice was fighting for a space to be heard through my confused thoughts. Dazed, exhausted, my eyes swollen with tears, I slowly turned, silently obeying his instructions. I tried to focus through the kaleidoscope of my mind. I yearned to shake this bad dream that enveloped me. All of my illusions of reality had vanished. If there was a definition of Hell - this could be it!

My head felt like it was in a big bass drum with someone pounding on it to the rhythm of my heart. The large white doors ahead of me appeared distorted, as if I was looking at them through the bottom of a drinking glass. I had tunnel vision. Nothing was as it should be. The corridor walls were closing in on me while the ominous doors appeared to be alive; waiting to devour me as I walked closer towards them. Once I entered into their realm would I ever be able to return, or would I be delivered into obscurity? I could hear the nurse breathing somewhere behind me. He called himself a nurse but I knew he was also a guard, an evil angel sent to deliver me into this place of eternal damnation.

Was I breathing? Were my feet even touching the floor? Everything seemed surreal, frightening, and constant pounding in my head grew louder and began to be accompanied by voices laughing and screaming 'You're doomed, you're doomed.'

My eyes focused on the sign above the foreboding doors. The words terrified me. I stopped. I wanted to turn and run but I didn't know where to go, so I just stood there looking at the sign, desperately looking for answers and finding none. When I felt a firm hand on my shoulder I knew it was over. This hand would not let me go. Reluctantly I walked through the doors with the sign above them that read "Psychiatric Ward."

Powerless, no longer in command of my body, my soul gone to a place I had no knowledge of, I lumbered through the doors. Once inside, the hand on my shoulder forced me to stop. I listened as the doors slowly closed behind me, laughing in their victory. To my right, an office with thick windows was manned by more of these white clad creatures. The one that brought me walked over and spoke to a female of the species. They were forever moving closer - further away, closer - further away. Had they drugged me? Where did my world go? What had taken over my body and soul?

Then my guard nurse returned and directed me down another hallway until we reached another door. This one was open and he directed me to enter. More white walls, a couple of chairs, and a bed awaited me inside. I was given hospital pyjamas and told to put all of my clothing in a bag provided. He left me alone for a moment while I complied. A few moments later he returned, gave me a pill, took my bag of clothes and left. With him went the last of what was me. No clothes, no wallet, no belt, I stood looking out of the large window, dressed in my hospital pyjamas. Out there was a world I no longer comprehended or belonged to.

When I looked to my right I could see, far off in the distance, the neighbourhood where my common-law wife and children lived. With them I once had it all: love, a house, respect, even my own business. Then came the recession; Stocks crashed, interest rates soared and overnight I lost my business. I had to get a job and fast. I suffered a reality shock and woke up broke. It became harder and harder to look my wife and children in the face.

To my left I could see where the girl I had cheated with lived and wondered how it had come to be that I could desire her so, to be obsessed by her to the point of not being able to see beyond her. It didn't matter who I hurt or why. I had left my wife and children for her and when I told her what I had done, and that we could be together whenever we wanted, she no longer wanted me.

For two days I hardly ate. I cried, I slept, I gazed out of the window to my left and to my right and I cried some more.

Every day I met with a psychiatrist. Outside of that I was basically left alone to try to work things out my own way. My main prescription was rest, and pills if I needed them to help me sleep. After a week they gave me back my clothes. I had permission to go outside for fresh air, provided I did not leave the hospital grounds. Misbehaviour would lead to loss of privileges. There were daily group sessions and I was allowed visitors. My wife came to see me once then stated that she would not be back because she could not stand to see me in this environment.

In the beginning of my second week I felt aggressive. The

duty nurse was advised and I was accompanied into a room thinking I was going to be interviewed, or strapped to a bed until I calmed down. Instead I discovered a punching bag in the corner of the room. The nurse taped my hands and helped me put on boxing gloves. She told me to go to the bag and punch it. I walked over and feeling stupid, I hit it lightly. I was told to hit it harder. I hit it once, and then again.

The next thing I remember I was on my knees, crying and striking the bag with what little strength I had left. The nurse told me to stop. I was exhausted, drenched in sweat, and when she removed the gloves blood stained the tape. My knuckles were bleeding as a result of my efforts. The nurse told me she had never seen anyone hit the bag so hard, and for so long. (One-and-a-half hours) She asked questions but I had no idea who I was trying to punch or why. (Today I realize I was striking out at myself.) Three days later, I was released as an outpatient. I got an apartment near where my wife and children lived and returned to doing what I knew best. I got a job driving.

But that is not where the story ends. When I got into my truck and began driving I embarked on a road and I had no idea where it would end or how. I had no inclination of what was waiting for me on the outside. One thing I do know is: when God decides he wants you – watch out.

Later, I moved to another city. I got into the habit of praying every day and going to mass. I even became caretaker of my parish church which gave me time to sit alone and contemplate the issue of God. Eventually I began to visit the parish priest once a week for an hour to discuss questions I had about my faith. He proved to be a wonderful and understanding mentor. Though life has since cast us in different directions, I still miss the conversations we had.

During the week I drove my truck all night and slept during the day. This gave me no time to think of much else and I spent all of the time alone. During this time I would contemplate God and the Bible and I would pray. The world became my church. The sky was the roof. The hills and the trees were the walls, while the ground and the road I drove on was the floor. The birds and animals, along with passing motorists became the congregation as I began to look upon the world in a new light. Distant lightning, starlit skies, snowstorms and autumn winds; I saw it all through my windshield. I was never lonely. For me it was the best time of my life. No one to answer to; I didn't have to prove anything to anyone, I didn't have to please or perform for anybody, nor did I have to distance myself from my true feelings. I could just be me.

I became an armchair philosopher, *only my armchair was usually travelling at 100+kph.* I could openly contemplate God, Mary, the Bible, or anything else and there was no-one around to call me down. I began to speak to God and Mary – if they answered I didn't hear it, but I did feel closer to them. *(Maybe that's how they answer)* I guess my prayers became my thoughts, and my thoughts became my prayers.

I continue to pray and contemplate throughout my day. The other day it came to my mind that although I say the word "God" I've been thinking only of Jesus and neglecting God the father and creator of all things. I pray thinking of Jesus, the Holy Spirit and Mary. Sometimes I pray to St. Joseph to intercede for me, but I have not been thinking of God the father. Even when I pray the 'Our Father', the prayer that Jesus taught us, I've been thinking of Jesus. I'm sure this is not wrong, and I don't want to diminish my adoration of Jesus, yet, as I think of Jesus on earth, all the time he was here, didn't he build up his father to us without thought of himself? Didn't he always speak of the father and pray to the father? Weren't the miracles he performed for the glorification of the father? And wasn't it he who taught us the 'Our Father'? I'm not trying to preach here. Everybody already knows what I am saying. It's just that without changing my love or my beliefs in Jesus or my devotion to Mary, I feel I've just been introduced to the Creator, God the father as I write this and it's like a light just went off in my head.

I remember when I was reintroduced to my son. Although I always knew of him I didn't know him, nor did he know me. We'd been separated for 25 years. I remember how I felt when I first went to meet him. I was scared but very anxious to see him. When I first laid eyes on him the bonding was immediate and I was overwhelmed with love and pride that I had such a son. All the years of knowing that there was something missing in my life and in my heart, the endless feeling of emptiness, like a part of me was missing, disappeared in one moment as we shook hands that first day. As it was with my son it was and is an exciting time for me again since I met God my father for the first time last week. Now when I look back at things I've already written I can see that sometimes I was writing about God, without really thinking about him.

As I continued in my quest to discover my faith, life didn't get any easier. The temptations of the world were the same for me as for most others. At first, I still enjoyed my weekend lifestyle of wine, women and song. However, as time passed after my separation, and my quest for my faith continued to grow, I began to be drawn towards a new path. Some will understand when I say that more and more I felt like an object expected to perform. It was as if that was the main, if not the sole purpose of a relationship. I loved being alone in my truck during the week because I had no time to visit with anyone as I drove all night while everyone was sleeping, and slept all day while everyone worked. As Friday approached I began to feel like most people feel on Monday. I dreaded to see Saturday come. Often I just wanted to spend a weekend alone but I couldn't resist. By then I had another girlfriend and I wasn't ready to break it off.

Then, about one year after our separation, my ex called and asked if I was interested in going to a weekend religious conference. I didn't hesitate. *(At this point I should mention that even though my ex and I remained friends we never again entered into a relationship of any kind.)* While there, I met a Nun who had given a lecture and she asked if I would like to visit her mixed community in the province of Quebec. The convent's mission was to assist youth. I agreed and spent a few weekends there. Then I decided, with the guidance of the Nun, to give up my job and join the convent as a volunteer. It would be the decisive moment that changed my life.

For the next two years, I spent my time lecturing in schools with the Nun and other members of the community. I spent time in classes given by the Nun, and going to religious group meetings where I listened to speakers of different walks of life. I enjoyed the education I got and was happy in that environment. Then, about two years later, I fell and broke my foot. There was no place to stay at the community as they were moving to a new location and had no one to care for me. So, being obedient to the wishes of the leaders, I returned to heal at my parents' home. I continued to pray and the good sister came to visit from time to time to see how I was doing. By the time my foot healed, and after numerous conversations with the Nun and others, I finally decided it was time I left the community and returned to driving.

My religious education did not end there, for as I travelled across the U.S.A. and Canada I met many spiritual drivers and had many conversations. Some of the subjects follow.

The Bible

I discovered that the Bible is a precious gift written by humans, but dictated by God. It's not a book that can or should be read like any other book. It's a book to be lived, contemplated and searched in order to find answers in our lives. It's been read, studied by the scholars, printed and reprinted and translated into every language in the world. It has been interpreted in more ways than can be counted. In some cases it has been altered to fit the follower's needs. There have been accusations that it's false or that it's no more than a fantasy book for the poor and feeble. It is sometimes said that it was written for times that have passed and that it, or parts of it, no longer apply today. People have lived by it, judged and been judged by it, laughed at it, tried to destroy it, rejected it, profited by it and died for it. Yet, despite all, it continues to be found in the possession of all types of people, from all walks of life, in all parts of the world.

Where the Bible was made illegal by the rulers of countries, people memorized different parts of it and did this at their own peril and often, at risk of death, they gathered in secret places to recite the words they knew so the word of God could be shared. Numerous persons of all denominations have perished delivering the word of God.

I sincerely believe in the word of the Bible. I believe all of it is true, for if one part of it is not true then how can any of it be true? I believe it's written not for a time but for all time, or else it might as well remain on the bookshelf in a museum along with other souvenirs as a reminder of an unforgettable time, in days gone by, that we cherish and miss like a first love or a first kiss that is always remembered but never returns.

I believe it is written so as to be interpreted by each soul. As we are all individuals unlike any other, so is our path different. Thus, if the Bible is one of the ways God speaks to us as individuals then so must be its interpretation. Does this mean we should just go off and be on our own disregarding all else?

I would suggest this might be very foolish indeed. Did not

God also create and give us our religious leaders, our scholars, our lawyers, our politicians, etc.? Don't we all have a
role to play in the workings of the world? I think interpreting
the Bible without the guidance of others is as dangerous as
performing heart surgery on one's self. Without the guidance
of the official interpretation and the teachings of our leaders
how would it be possible to form a reasonable individual understanding of what we read and learn? *For example, I offer
that when one works and gets paid that person is responsible
for the money earned: however, how wise could the person be
with his pay if no one had taught him at least some basics of
math?*

I also don't believe one should put all of their eggs in one
basket. (Old cliché) As far as I know, God gave us all a brain
and a curious disposition. Yes, he sends people to guide us
and yes, he gives them that which is needed to do so. We may
not all have the same guide. For example, the guide God has
in mind for my wife may not be the one he has in mind for
me. Yet, God does not stop me from speaking with her guide.
There may also be a third guide to assist the two of us together. Guides could be our minister, other religious leaders, or
someone else.

What God does, if I want to listen, is to put in my heart
what is right for me and what isn't. The key is to listen, above
all else, to what one believes God is saying. Sounds easy,
but it's very hard, since God speaks to us in whispers, like
a soft summer breeze that can be felt but neither heard nor
seen, and yet it cools and soothes those who are working or
playing hard while it remains undetected to those who are
sitting idle.

Then again, it's not for me to ignore what my wife's guide
says. On the contrary, by combining what my wife, my
friends, and even what strangers believe with all that I have
learned and have faith in, I may perhaps have a better chance
of coming closer to the truth God has for me. Prayer of any
type is always good when it comes from the heart. Although
in the beginning Prayer may not come from the heart – but
who knows, perhaps in time it will find its way to the heart.

Taking into account all of the above, I meditated over
parts of the Bible that came to mind. I use Love as the main

theme, I look at what is written in the Bible and what is in the Bible by omission. I ask how this can affect my life today. Christ spoke in parables so as to inspire thought, thought causes study *(meditation is a form of study)* and study leads to learning. I soon discovered the Bible is for all time and it does apply to me today. I found a loving friend and father in God, Jesus and the Bible. Then God gave me a very special gift. **I discovered that it is alright to be me.**

I write these pages so that I might remember from time to time this precious gift I have been given. Also, so that in the best of times as well as the worst of times, no matter where life brings me, I'll remember that God is love and we are of God, thus, we are a part of his love.

Genesis

'In the beginning' is how some Bibles start, while others say 'On the first day' God created the heavens and the stars and continues to describe the order in which he created Heaven and Earth and all that exists. Finally he created man and from his rib created woman. *(Adam and Eve)* On the seventh day God rested.

Already arguments occur. Science shows that it took millions – or is it billions of years to create the universe and all that exists. It began with two or more molecules colliding and expanded from there so God didn't create everything in seven days. This might make sense, and who am I to say that science isn't true? What does it change? God gives us the order in which all was created. He speaks to us in terms we can understand. If he spoke to us in his terms, it would be like a university professor trying to explain the workings of the space shuttle using scientific language and equations, while speaking to preschool students.

In the beginning, on the first day, or two billion years ago, time is relevant to space and where we stand in the universe. Science itself tells us that on some planets a day is much shorter than that of the earth while on other planets a day is as long as two earth weeks. How long is a day to the eternal God, who has no beginning and no end? Or can one imagine the size of the book it would take to write in detail all of God's creation? God, it seems to me, gives us what we need and lets us figure out the rest. Thus, with what God has given us we continue to discover the mysteries of his creation. After millions of years we are just scratching the surface of all the amazing things there are to discover in creation. In God's love, I believe he wants us to search and discover. Would that not be one of the reasons he gave us intelligence - to seek out the truth?

I love science and technology. The other day I watched a documentary I found to be extremely interesting. A scientist showed the earth and the universe. He showed ancient discoveries on earth that demonstrated how humans were quite intelligent for longer than I ever thought. And he showed the universe. He explained the supernovas, how they come about and what happens as a result. Then the program demonstrated how the entire universe began with the colliding of molecules that split and continued to split and multiply over billions of years. He then showed how the universe is also going to, over billions of years, burn itself out and disappear so that there will be nothing left. What we now see as a majestic universe will be one big void. The earth, he explained, will be gone long before that and our sun will have its own supernova long before the final star vanishes.

Wow, I just can't fathom all of those accidents causing such wonderment as exist today. To think of accidents causing all of the rules of science, technology and physics of the universe is definitely out of my scope. Who am I to disagree with this study? What confuses me is:

Where did the first two molecules come from? Everyone knows that even molecules have a life span *(a beginning and an end)* How did they come to be if before them there was an absolute void? Since science has proven without doubt that the universe has a beginning and an end, somewhere, sometime, somehow, didn't something have to kick start it from nothing?

How did an infinity of microscopic accidents cause a tree to be, and then the accidents turned into rules stating that a tree cannot of its own accord be anything else but a tree? And not just a tree but a Maple tree can only be a Maple tree and cannot become a Spruce tree etc.?

How is it that everything in the universe functions by a set of rules from which it cannot normally deviate. Every plant and animal has a specific purpose in caring for the earth's garden and when outside intervention sways the balance it can endanger large portions of the earth to the point of making it uninhabitable?

How is it that the human race is the only exception to this rule and that we are the only species on earth with the power to govern over all of the other animals, plants and food sources of the planet to insure it's health and prosperity? We are the only species to know we are alive, that we were born, and we will die. We make choices, love, hate and we are the only ones with the power to seek out truth, cures for ailments and so on, and so on. How many molecular accidents did it take to make us and when did the accidents become rules – for without intervention, a human can only be a human.

Acting in faith, for I admit: I have not studied much on the subject; I believe the universe was created by a vast series of events. I am not, however, convinced all was an accident, moreso I am sure all was intentional and so my sentiments are reinforced as to the greatness of God Almighty. I believe even more in his infinite wisdom, love and patience. Science and technology make me know that God is gentle and caring. To each his own, and without saying anyone is wrong I merely state that as far as I'm concerned, until the day a man or woman can go into outer space and stand in a void without any form of artificial support or clothing, cup his or her hands together while holding absolutely nothing, whisper a breath into his or her hands and create even the smallest molecule to begin a new world, I will continue to believe in the creator with all of my heart and without doubt. To me all else is discovery, not creation.

II

The Bible says God created man, Adam, to be in charge of his creation. Then, seeing that Adam was lonely, God created Eve to be his partner. He created them equal. At first all was well in the garden, and the only stipulation by God was that they not eat the fruit of the forbidden tree. There are those that would argue whether or not it was a fruit tree, or whether the forbidden fruit was sex.

I believe the Bible tells us that when God created Adam and Eve he told them to go forth and procreate. If this is true then I would suggest sex was not the forbidden fruit. As far as what kind of fruit it was - what does it change?

Isn't the main issue the fact that they disobeyed God by doing whatever it was that was forbidden? Isn't the rest secondary? Don't these insignificant arguments lead us astray from what the Bible is trying to teach? If it's that hard to agree on what they did, then let's just agree they disobeyed and focus on the significance of their disobedience.

When God looked for Adam and Eve the next morning he found them hiding in the bush. Asked why he was hiding, Adam says he was naked and ashamed. God asks who told you that you were naked. God dressed Adam and Eve and now we believe being naked except when necessary is a sin and shameful.

I believe the Bible says God saw they were ashamed and clothed them. Then he tells them the results of their original sin – growing old, dying, suffering, working for food, pain in birth etc. I would suggest they also learned the feelings they did not know before. *(Lust, hate, envy, deceit, and all that is against love).* Does this mean that all of these things are punishment for their sin, or are they part of the other side of knowledge they gained?

I would suggest as a result of their disobedience Adam and Eve were with sin and thus God's relationship with them changed. I was taught that after this the gates of Heaven were closed to our souls until God's son Jesus Christ redeemed us. It seems to me, as I contemplate the subject, that death and the diminished relationship with God was, and is perhaps the punishment. As far as the rest goes, God might have been informing Adam and Eve of the results of the human condition they acquired when they ate of the 'fruit of knowledge.'

In another example, if a parent tells his child he can go play outside but he is not to climb a tree, what happens when the child thinks he is alone and climbs the tree? The child falls and suffers cuts and bruises. The father, when he discovers the disobedience sends the boy to his room for an hour. Are the cuts and bruises part of the father's punishment for climbing the tree or merely a result of the forbidden adventure while not heeding the father's warning? The father, knowing his son could get hurt, told him not to climb the tree, but isn't the only punishment the hour the child spent in the room? Are not the cuts and bruises a part of what the father tried to avoid for his child?

God also said woman will tempt and seduce man but this does not mean all women do so or that they have to do so. I cannot find any instance where God left us with described actions, without leaving us choice.

I would submit that 'man will dominate woman' is also not a rule from God nor is it a must, as some are lead to believe. To me that is just an interpretation made by humans in order to dominate other humans. God, knowing we as humans would behave like this, merely advised us of what the future held. I believe, and submit to you, that when God says something or gives us something he does not change his mind or take it away. In the beginning, God said man and woman would be one equal partner governing over the land and all living things. I am convinced that he did not go back on his word. We, after the original sin, did not accept and keep his word.

Sin

Sin, a very small word yet I have failed to find a word more complex, powerful and confusing. It is a word most often used in a religious atmosphere as the main if not the only reason for the existence of hell.

As a young boy, I remember my first fear was of the darkness. Alone in my darkened room, a partially opened closet door, a curtain blowing gently in an evening breeze, or the underside of my bed were all places where a monster lurked just waiting to devour me. Any moving shadow was for sure the boogie man coming for me.

I remember once when my parents were visiting friends, I was sleeping in the same room as my older brother. At the foot of his bed a blanket with a black line in it was folded in anticipation of colder nights. My brother silently moved his feet under the blanket. In my childhood imagination the moving black line was a never ending snake crawling over his bed and heading towards mine. I eventually fell asleep exhausted; terrified this snake was going to swallow me. Fears like this only lasted for a few years before I was old enough to know the difference. Only in certain circumstances like being alone in the forest or a lonely street at night did this fear return. This fear I could of course eliminate with reasoning.

Then, as I started attending school and Sunday school I began to learn about God and sin. Out came the rules and commandments that if I failed to obey, the devil, portrayed as an ugly human-like creature with horns and a big pitchfork surrounded by fire, would come and take me to his home in hell where I would live and burn for all eternity.

The list of sins one could commit was ever-growing and seemed to involve just about everything I did even at that young age. The list of good things one should do seemed to diminish and become almost impossible to accomplish. I remember trying to be good but inevitably I would do something wrong like disobeying my parents or swearing and again I would be afraid of the devil. I soon gave up on the church, feeling sure it was useless and that I was irreversibly doomed for hell. The influences of the church, my Christian parents and society kept me in this shell of impending doom until I was a man in my thirties. One example is that as a young man living alone I decided to sleep nude. The resulting feeling was almost the same as when I was very young. I felt that if I should die that night I was surely doomed for hell. I could almost feel the devil coming for me. My education was that one could only be nude in the bath or shower, or very briefly while changing clothing, and never in the presence of persons of the opposite sex unless married.

––––––––

Later in life, as I drove my truck, listening to the Bible on audio cassette or listening to different radio evangelists throughout the U.S. and Canada and combining this with the teachings of my church and the religious community I lived in for two years, I began to meditate on the subject of sin. It soon became apparent to me that this is a very complicated and complex subject. One of my first conclusions was that God must be a very busy god.

If sin were categorized in a law book for instance there would be so many books it would take more library shelves than there are for parliamentary law books. The sin and justice department would fill more than one office tower and the staff to sort it all out would outnumber any government offices I know.

I was privileged enough to have been raised in two cultures: French and English. As I thought of these two cultures, I realized that there were many things I could say and do in one culture that were fine, but if I did the same thing in the other culture it was a sin. I did not take the time to study other cultures but I believe it's all the same. I understand that in some cultures taking more than one wife is permitted. Killing another human being is a mortal sin yet some places have the death penalty for murders and that is not a sin. Soldiers are sent to war where bombs are dropped while people shoot and stab each other. However as long as one is fighting 'on the side of God' it's not a sin. The trouble is all soldiers believe they are on the side of God.

Looking into the realm of religion each faith has its own set of do's and don'ts. A Catholic cannot divorce and can only marry once unless the other partner dies. Any Catholic who does divorce and remarries is therefore living in sin. Those adhering to Protestant religions can, however, divorce and remarry in their church without fear of living in sin. Prostitutes are banned from most churches but not from their customers. The list goes on and on. Imagine God in Heaven when people die? You were Catholic, divorced and remarried – so you can't come in. You were Protestant, divorced and re-married? Come on in. You spoke English and said this word or that word? You can't come in. You said the same word in another language, so that's all right. You didn't go to church . . . You wore a hat . . . You didn't pay your dues . . .

It sure boggled my mind. I began to laugh at the thought of it all. I thought of God looking down at us with patient understanding and thinking of how we sure like to complicate our lives. The truth is one of those mysteries we will discover when we finally get to heaven. Until then, we can only contemplate, meditate, speculate and philosophize on the true meaning of the word.

To me, it seems reasonable that if there is a God who is love and there is a Hell, which is the absence of love, then there must be bad if there is good. Yet, what is sin? If sin exists then it must be an act against God and if it is an act against God then it must be an act against love. If love exists, then sin also exists, for if sin does not exist then love does not exist. Thus God and Hell do not exist. All must be true and intertwined or none of it exists.

Is a sin, therefore, not in what we do but why we do it? If one kills another out of hate, jealousy or vengeance etc. then that act is not done out of love and is probably a sin. But, if a person destroys another life because it is the only option that will save other lives then that is an act of love for the lives saved and is probably not a sin.

I've known some people who professed not to believe in God, yet they devoted their lives to their wives and children, worked hard and gave all to better the lives of those they loved. Without question they came to the aid of those in need and taught their children to love and respect others. Never did I hear a disrespectful word exit their mouths. I have a hard time believing that God will send these people to eternal damnation because they say they don't believe in him. More so I believe that because they are capable of such love they will be welcomed by love.

On the other hand I have known Christians who have been just the opposite. In fact some of the non-believers I have known admitted that it was because of the actions of some Christians that they did not believe.

In my reflections I found it very hard to believe that if God is love he would refuse to give his love to a soul, not because of lack of love, but because he/she said they did not believe. I think that after death, the person would recognize love and therefore recognize God and adore him. I wonder who would be more receptive to eternal love, one who takes marriage vows but never honors them or one who does not take marriage vows but lives by the laws of love and marriage with their partner throughout their lives?

I've committed more sins than I'll ever be able to count. I believe Jesus saved me, and not because I deserve it in any way. If I did not believe this, then what would be the purpose of even trying to live a good life? My closet is full of skeletons, as I suppose most closets are. There is, however, an example of my sins that I really have trouble with. What I consider a real act against love and possibly the worst sin I ever committed.

One day I was in town in the middle of summer and stopped at a French-fry wagon to purchase a hot dog and fries. As I sat on a bench to eat a homeless man came up to me and asked for money to buy some fries. I told him I had none; the truth is I didn't have much. The man looked at me and said he would get some fries without my help. He walked a little ways away from me and proceeded to ask passersby for money. Once in a while he would look at me and holler that he would get some fries and that he didn't need me. Eventually I got upset and lost my temper. I threw the box holding the few fries I had left on the ground in his direction while screaming that if he wanted fries there they were! Then I got up and walked away.

Unequivocal Love

When I calmed down, I realized what I had done. For the longest time and even to this day I sometimes look for this man when I'm in town. If I ever found him I would apologize, though I doubt he'd remember after all these years, and then I would buy him a big order of fries and include a burger and cola. Of all the sins I have committed this is the one that holds me in a firm grip. I, to date, cannot forgive myself for this action and pray to God to forgive me and help that homeless man. My trust in God is that he will. This to me was a real act against love and a real sin.

Sin to me is not an act against one religion or another but an act, for the most part, against love. God gave us Ten Commandments in the Old Testament. In the New Testament, Jesus made it even easier for us by combining these into two commandments:

The common denominator in these commandments is Love. If one does their best to live by love, then perhaps one is less prone to sin and more apt to be able to accept God's Love and to love God.

Judgment

I try to imagine God ruling as we would. Our sins would be met with such things as shoot him, hang him, sue her, deport her, or lock them in jail, etc. Twenty years on a third strike, civil suit after criminal trial *(guilty or not)*, in some countries death and dismemberment are permanent consequences of even the most menial of crimes. Because God does not 'follow our lead' we accuse him of being unjust, cruel, and we turn away from him and deny his existence.

An image comes to my mind where I am being tried in court and as I look around I see the jurors are all five-year-old children. This image tells me of the results of trying to bring God down to our size. Yes, laws are important. Yes, there have to be consequences for the disruption of society, and yes, there has to be a code of acceptable conduct in all societies, otherwise we have chaos. In most societies, one is judged without hate or malice but one is also judged without love. On earth we are judged by whatever amount of truth and scientific proof we wish to seek out. It's the best we have but is it God's way?

We judge people by their ethnic backgrounds, by the clothes they wear or how they speak. Are they rich or are they poor? Do they go to the same church as I, or do they go to church at all? Why do they let their child stay out so late? Why don't they let their child go out to play? Doesn't he think he's something? She's just a little tramp. And it goes on and on. That person's too big. This one's too skinny. Whatever happened to 'judge not lest you be judged'. Are we now judging ourselves for our eternal rewards by the way we are judging others? Is it mirroring back to us?

We judge our neighbors by the car they drive and when they arrive one day with a new car that looks nicer than ours we become jealous. Suddenly our neighbors are snobs, arrogant, showoffs etc. Isn't it funny how words like jealousy are associated with the word judgment? In a list both words would appear on the side against love.

What about in court when someone sits before a 'Judge' to be judged by a jury as to whether they are guilty or not guilty of a crime. I believe the 'Judge' is a misrepresentation of the person's title. He/she should be named President or CEO of the court. The 'Judge's' job is not to judge the accused but to preside over the trial and insure all is conducted in accordance with the laws of the land. If the accused is found guilty, the judge then assigns punishment. But at no time does the judge himself (or herself) judge the person on trial. The judge would probably be charged with misconduct in such a case.

The jury doesn't judge the prisoner, either. Jurors listen to all the evidence and simply decide if the person is guilty or not guilty of a crime. They in no way pass judgment over the person. They simply make a ruling after reviewing all the facts presented, regarding guilt or innocence. Anything more would be out of order.

The lawyers don't judge either. They debate both sides of a case to the jury who decides the conclusion. So, if a person or persons of any race, or religious denomination can go to court for anything from a parking ticket to mass murder and not be judged, why can't a person get through a day without being judged for skin color, language, or the way he or she dresses, or even the people they speak with?

When I was in my mid-teens, I met a girl at a dance whom I had known years before. Of course, I was drunk that night when I asked her to dance, but she accepted. After the dance I returned to sit with my friends, at which time I was told she was a lesbian. My friends all laughed but I didn't. Drunk as I was, I didn't dance with her again either. I now know my friends were joking around. In their drunken stupor, they thought it was funny. Meanwhile, I'll never know what might have been if I hadn't listened to them. I don't blame them or their judgment of her. I blame myself for not being strong enough to ignore them and go my own way, but then again, I believe everything happens for a reason.

Submission

The Bible says a woman must be submissive to her husband. It has been a sore spot within the church since I was old enough to remember and I often watched as religious leaders stumbled to answer the questions of women over the issue. In other cases, some cults use it to gain male dominance over women. I contemplated many years over the issue as I drove up and down the North American highways and could not match up submission and equality in the same sentence.

Then I watched a movie *(I believe the title was Take the Lead)* about a dance teacher who teaches a group of troubled students to dance as a way to come out of their shell. At one point he tells a young lady she must let the young man lead her and she refuses, asking why she should have to submit to him. *(Not an exact quote)* The instructor's answer caught my attention more than any other part of the movie. He said something like this: *(again not an exact quote)*

When the woman submits to her partner, she leads by submission. In other words, she gives him permission to lead her to the place of happiness and security that she expects him to take her to in the dance.

It didn't take much to relate that statement to the Bible. When a woman submits to her partner, does she not also lead by submission? Does she not give him permission to lead her to the place of happiness and security she expects in their relationship for her and their children?

The actor also stated that *when the man accepts to lead he promises to lead the woman to the place of security and happiness she expects in the dance;* thereby submitting to her.

It didn't take much to relate that statement to the Bible. When the man accepts to lead in the partnership doesn't he promise to submit to her and promise to abandon all else in order to lead his partner to the place of happiness and security she expects of him? And in return isn't she expected to devote herself, as an equal partner, to the relationship?

If, for example, the man drinks, gambles and squanders

the family budget and such, therefore failing in his 'leadership' roll *(as described above)* does it become the woman's duty to submit to her partner by:

Sitting by quietly and watching him destroy everything they worked for while letting their children go without? Or

Does it become part of her submissive roll, not to sit and watch the destruction, but to take over and secure the budget and the family however she can?

When all is said and done, isn't submission to each other a submission of the heart (a submission of love, forsaking all others in the eyes of God and man) and not a physical entity? When we read the part that says for wives to submit themselves do we forget the part that reads – *as unto the lord.*

If we quit repeating – wives submit yourselves – which takes on a physical form, and we begin to concentrate on the last part – as unto the lord – then I would suggest the term submission takes on a spiritual form in God's love and speaks not of the physical.

God, I believe, did not create slaves. Mankind did in order to feed their lust for power and riches. I suggest that we, over time, have taken what is meant to be a rich, fulfilling spiritual experience between husband and wife and turned it into some way of gaining dominance over another human being. (Which I believe to be distasteful to God)

The last sentence in St. Paul's instructions to 'husbands and wives' states that man should love his wife as himself and the woman should treat their spouse with reverence. (Reverence – is religious respect usually held for clergy) Nowhere in St. Paul's instructions to man do I see where man is to do anything but love and respect his wife – *as Christ loved his church.* I would suggest that the submission is a spiritual submission of love by both the man and woman to love – as we are submitted to God's love.

Hell

I begin to ask myself about Hell and the punishment for those without love, those who reject God's love and those whose sole purpose is to hurt and cause hardship. Who they are I do not know and, try not to judge. I don't have to; God is there to do that if and when necessary. But what if there are those who need to be judged?

For as long as I can remember I've been told hell was a place of fire and brimstone where we burned forever. This caused me to wonder, since after death my body will be reduced to ashes and then nothing. Cremated bodies, for instance, don't feel pain. I am told the soul has no nerves and it isn't a physical entity, so how would fire and brimstone hurt it in any way? I couldn't figure it out, but it didn't scare me much. It sounded too much like someone's imagination running wild or like one of those science fiction stories on TV or in the theatres.

As a child, every time I turned around I was being threatened with hell. Priests and preachers and other religious experts were always saying to repent or I would burn in hell. Pictures showed this terrible monster with a pitchfork and horns just waiting to bring me into his realm of fire and pain. Every time someone read the Bible, hell was there if I didn't do what it said. For the longest time, it seemed that no matter what I did, I was doomed to hell. The only alternative was to ignore all of my earthly feelings and spend 24 hours a day praying.

If I ate too much, I was a glutton destined for hell, but if I ate too little or left food on my plate I was wasteful and going to the same place. If I didn't look at girls there was something wrong, but if I did look at them I was lustful and you guessed it, Hell-bound. If I didn't listen to my parents etc. etc.... Hell-bound. That big nasty creature with the horns was coming to get me. Even today, although as a rule things have changed, I still hear preachers "scaring us with hell".

Yet, now I ask myself, "are fear and threats a part of love? What role do they play in love? I know I don't feel loved when someone tries to scare or threaten me. I feel more like they are trying to get something from me, or to intimidate me with these tactics. All too often I've discovered the answer usually comes with a dollar sign. I'm convinced fear and threats have no part in God's love and, therefore, I become leery if these tactics are used in any walk of life.

When I look at all that God has done for us, his creations, the world, the stars, the planets, the weather, the animals, nature in general, we ourselves, a newborn, there's no way I can conceive that all this was done so we could be threatened and scared to finally burn in hell. Any God that would act in such a way is definitely not my God of love.

Nor do I believe God is some sort of sugar daddy and I can do all I want and still go to heaven to be with him. He sent us Jesus who died for our sins and therefore I'm saved: no question about it. But isn't it up to me to accept the fact that I'm saved? Isn't it up to me to want to be saved? Isn't it up to me to act as if I'm saved, or to reject being saved? God in his love leaves me with the choice to accept or refuse his gift of love and eternal happiness. If God gives me this choice then there must be an option to choose from. If I don't accept him as my savior and reject his love, then because my soul is eternal, there must be somewhere else for me. Thus I came to the conclusion that Hell must exist.

Hell cannot be a happy place because God offers eternal happiness in heaven. Yet it cannot be a painful place since I will be unable to feel physical pain. So how can it be possible for me to suffer the most unendurable pain I have ever felt? My thoughts turned to a conversation I had with a religious leader many years ago concerning Hell and suffering. His comments in response to my questions went somewhat as follows:

What if the pain is not physical? Where does love come from? That is to say, the feeling of love? Pain, physical pain comes from our nervous system which sends a message to our brain advising us of a problem with our body through signals we call pain.

Love, however, affects just about every part of our body making some parts feel week, other parts jittery or nervous etc., while our heart seems to beat faster and yet it seems to stop and we can't think straight. Doing silly things unusual to our normal character is not uncommon when we fall in love and our internal happiness reaches its peak.

Unlike when we feel physical pain, we cannot go to the doctor for a physical examination and have test results tell us we are in love, nor can we see it in x-rays. We feel love in our hearts yet no tests can show results pointing to the exact location where love begins. The reason for this is that the emotion of love is not physical. Though it affects our physical being, it does not generate from any physical part of our body. Love and falling in love is at best only partially controllable. A good love often leads to years of happiness while a bad love often leads to mistrust and hatred.

"Imagine that when you die your soul lives on and goes before God," the priest said.

"When you see God, you see pure, perfect eternal love and happiness. Think of the happiest love you ever experienced. Not sexual love but real deep love of someone or something in your life and the pleasure being with that person or thing gave you. Multiply this by a million-fold. The pleasure of such a love would be unimaginable. This endless love might be Heaven.

"Now imagine this again, but this time, what if you can see this immeasurable love, but as bad as you want it you can't have or partake in it. You know the love is there, you see the love but there is an invisible wall or object stopping you from sharing in it.

"Remember the first person you loved and how they didn't love you in return," the priest continued.

"Remember the pain of seeing that person in love with someone other than you. Remember the pain when they laughed or held hands, or especially if you saw them kiss. Didn't the pain, the frustration, the jealousy, the sorrow feel like it was unbearable and that you would surely die? Now," he said, "Multiply that pain by a million-fold. What if this is the suffering of Hell?"

God is love, God is eternal, and God created us and gave us a soul which is eternal. God promises us the eternal love and happiness of heaven. If we know love in eternity with God, I asked myself, can we not also, if we reject this love during our lifetime, know the suffering of the lack of love or the lack of access to such a perfect love in eternity. Surely, if God is love and Heaven is living in the purest form of love then Hell is perhaps the absence of love, living in the burning desire of knowing of love, wanting love but not being able to receive love. Imagine living in eternal hatred, jealousy, contempt, desire, suspicion, mistrust, deceit etc. Imagine the burning desire of unobtainable love. Now multiply that feeling to infinity.

Mary
(The Blessed Virgin)

Mary has been given many titles by Christians through-out time. The Virgin Mary, Mary Mother of God, and so on. The Bible tells us, and Christians believe she gave birth to Jesus in a manger, in Bethlehem. We all know the story of the angel announcing God's will to her, we know of her acceptance, the census, the trip to Bethlehem and the birth of Jesus in a manger but I can't help but wonder – who was Mary? The Bible tells us she was a virgin child and a pure and faithful servant of God. Did Mary know all of her child-hood life that one day she would give birth to Jesus?

It's Sunday. It's a quiet day. I've just listened to one of my Bible cassettes as I look at the scenery along the highway. I let my mind wander and I think of Mary, the Blessed Virgin. I think of my grandchildren, my friend's children and grand-children and I think of the children in the cars that pass me along this Sunday morning highway. Growing up, would Mary have been like them?

A young child, I think probably she would have played outside with her dolls just like any other child, then and now. Over time, her mother, Anne, would have begun to teach her things and assign her chores to do. Her father would have taught her of their faith and on the Sabbath they would have gone to the synagogue to worship God. No doubt, friends and relatives would have commented to her parents on what a lovely and obedient child she was. But did they know what her destiny was?

By the time she became a young lady, Mary's father had passed away. She lived with her mother and was betrothed *(or engaged)* to a fine young man named Joseph. Neither she, her mother, Joseph, nor the rest of the community had any idea of the events that were about to take place. Then the an-gel arrived with a message from God that changed the entire world forever. *(To put it in perspective, I thought of my com-munity. If such an event was about to happen again, would I know it?)*

Movies tend to show the arrival of the angels with gusting winds, howling dogs, vacant streets, and flapping shutters followed by rays of light shining through the window like a spotlight highlighting Mary. This is good dramatization and of course, in the movies, something has to happen so the audience knows what's going on, and maybe it did happen that way. I lean more towards the theory that God mostly comes to us like a whisper we really have to listen for in order to hear.

Another scenario might be that, saying her morning prayers, or lying quietly in bed, or maybe like a peaceful dream, a thought came to her mind and into her soul. Her questions may also have been just a thought in a peaceful half-sleep state of mind with absolutely no outward signs of the angel's presence.

I, on more than one occasion, have been in a half-sleep or dozing in and out of sleep. While in this relaxed state, I thought I was speaking with someone or an event was happening in my mind. When I became fully awake, what had been in my mind seemed very real. *(Like a half dream – I was speaking with my wife or a friend or something was happening.)* As I stated in an earlier chapter, I once dreamed the Virgin Mary appeared before me and told me to change my ways. Was this just a dream? I won't know until I die but I sometimes wonder what would have happened had I listened to the dream.

———————

Mary's encounter with the angel is a wonderful story of innocent faith and obedience as told. For a moment, I try to put myself in Mary's place. Today, there's no problem. A young lady can get pregnant without fear, married or not. Some ladies even prefer artificial insemination to having a husband or boyfriend. If a pregnancy is unwanted it can be terminated.

This was not the case for Mary, however. When Mary made her decision to accept God's plan, it was a very serious decision with possible extreme consequences. In Mary's day, an unwed mother could be sent away to have the child in shame. She, as well as her family, could be shamed and lose all of their possessions and any status they had in life. As well as being banished, she could cause her family to be sent into a state of poverty. She could suffer an "Honor killing' by her family or she would probably end up as a prostitute in order to survive.

Mary was betrothed to Joseph and as such, Joseph had the right, if she was unfaithful in any way, to cancel the nuptials and have her publicly shamed, or he could have her stoned to death for her infidelity. Did Mary know this when she said her **yes** to God? Undoubtedly, daughters were taught this at a very early age. What parent who knew of these dire consequences would not warn their child? Besides, wouldn't religion itself teach it? Knowing all of these risks, wanting to be a good daughter and honor her family name, and loving her fiancé Joseph, Mary still said yes to the angel without hesitation, fear or doubt. What if she had said no?

We're told Mary first told her mother Ann of the encounter with the angel. She was told as a sign of the word's significance that Elizabeth, Anne's sister whom they had not seen or heard of in a long while, was also with child.

I try to imagine what I'd do if my daughter approached me one morning and out of the blue announced she was pregnant with the Messiah. I'd probably be bringing her to a psychiatrist when she told me she was a virgin, her elder aunt was also pregnant and that she had to go to her.

Did Anne sit her daughter at the kitchen table and drill her about what had happened and who was the father, and was it Joseph and so on? From my meager resources all I can see is that she might have wondered about it but Anne didn't doubt her daughter. Knowing the possible consequences of Mary's condition, Anne did not condemn her daughter, but instead allowed her to go to Elizabeth.

In today's world, this would mean no more than a ticket on the bus, train, or plane if Mary didn't have a car. In Mary's day, things were quite different. A single lady could not travel alone and so Anne had to find or hire some older ladies to accompany her both as companions and witnesses to Mary's comportment while on the journey. Donkeys and/or camels would have to be hired to carry Mary, her maidens and the baggage. Then they would either form or join a caravan. Probably one or more men would have to be hired to protect the ladies as they travelled. Something would have had to be said to Joseph about Mary's Leaving. Did they lie to Joseph or did Anne decide to be vague until she received confirmation of Elizabeth's pregnancy?

In later years and even in our time there is much controversy about the Virgin Mary, most of which concerns her virginity. Was she a virgin? How long did she remain a virgin? I have heard arguments that if she was a virgin then Jesus would be some sort of half human beast. I have heard arguments that Mary was a virgin until death. Others have contended that she and Joseph lived a normal married life after the birth of Jesus. What does it matter? Do these arguments not serve only to cause division in the Christian churches of the world? Isn't Mary's giving birth to the baby Jesus the main issue? If the Christian communities could sort out the critical arguments as opposed to the divisional arguments of little consequence and agree to live together with our differences wouldn't we have a stronger worldwide community united in the love of God?

Joseph
(The expectant father)

It was a couple of weeks before Christmas and I didn't have a gift purchased, or any money to do my shopping with. My wife and I could hardly stand the emotional pain at the thought of disappointing our grandchildren and I had a hard time dealing with the sadness I saw in my wife's eyes.

I drove my truck feeling depressed and wondering how I might resolve the problem. At some point my thoughts turned to Joseph. Wasn't he just a man like me? A year earlier he was a young man working hard as a carpenter, engaged to a beautiful young lady, and dreaming of the day they would wed and settle down to raise a family. He had no idea of the events God had in mind for him. Then, in an instant his whole life changed. Now he was going to be a father and not just any father but father to the redeemer. Did he know what that meant or what was to come about?

How did he feel, I wondered, when he had to take his pregnant wife to Bethlehem for the census? He probably had some money with him but when he arrived he couldn't find a room for her. The rest of the world and the people gathered for the census didn't know who he was or even more important, they didn't know the child his wife was carrying. All the innkeepers knew was that this was a good opportunity for them to make lots of money selling their food and drinks and renting their rooms to the partying crowds. No innkeeper wanted the burden of a woman about to give birth.

So Joseph's search for a room failed. His money was of no use to him. How inadequate he must have felt watching his wife, whom he loved so dearly, suffering from labor pains in the street. Did he feel the frustration of failure as he stood not knowing what to do or where to go next? Did he feel then as I did now? Would he not have given everything he had to find a safe place for his wife to give birth? This couldn't have been his dream for his family. Surely he, as any father, had envisioned a good home and proper care for his wife when the moment of birth came. Would he not have worked hard and saved for the coming event? Yet, with all of his planning and preparation he had not anticipated the calling of the census at the exact time the baby would be due. Even he who knew his wife was carrying the Messiah probably had not given thought to the prophesy about the savior coming out of Bethlehem until the census was called. If he had would he not have gone ahead, or sent someone ahead of them to make preparations?

When Joseph ran out of options and was left not knowing what to do, God sent Abigail who showed them to a manger. A manger is just a type of barn with hay and animals and like all barns, no matter how clean they are, there's always clean hay and soiled hay. A young Joseph would surely have preferred a better place for the comfort of his wife and the birth of his child. Yet it seems the events were carrying him and his young family in a direction over which he had no control. Literature, and today's media depict Joseph as a man calmly doing God's will without thought or question, but to me it seems that if that were so then Joseph would have been deprived of his human freedom only to become a mere puppet of some superior being, demanding and controlling. This is not my vision or understanding of the teachings of God. Moreso, I believe God would have left Joseph with his normal humanity and Joseph would have had to make decisions and probably spent many sleepless nights wondering where events were taking them and if he were making the right decisions. I know of no humans that are always sure they are following the path God has planned for them. I would be surprised, if during his lifetime it was different for Joseph.

Once Joseph had the dream where the angel came to him and explained that it was God's will that Mary was with child, Joseph accepted apparently without further torment and from that moment on he became the caregiver of Christ on Earth. His was the responsibility to see to the child's welfare and education in the church. The angels spoke to him and told him when it was time to leave Bethlehem, when the king was dead, and when it was safe to return. Joseph was responsible to house and clothe and feed his family. Mary in the Bible steps back and assumes the mother's role of caring for the home and the child, as was the custom of the time. She observes the events in silence but for some years as the child grows they appear to live a normal life, raising, *to all appearances,* a gifted child. They were someone's next-door neighbors.

Joseph passed away when Jesus was of age to continue on his own, as if his mission on earth were complete and it was time to cede his place as head of the family to his eldest son.

The more I thought of Joseph the more I came to realize that before he became the saint he is he was just a man like me, and everybody else. He lived his life from day to day with hopes for the future and struggled through the daily problems and frustrations just as I did and as I was doing now. At that moment I offered the problems I was having to him and within a few days I had found, at least a temporary solution to my immediate problems which released some of the pressure from my wife and we did not disappoint our grandchildren. My problems are not all solved but the weight on my shoulders has been lessened since that day and I can't help feeling that if I could bring myself to give myself more to God, if I could only let go and allow him to take over, then my world would change. But that is easier said than done.

Throwing Stones

The New Testament tells of Jesus sitting near the wall of the city. A woman runs up to the wall chased by men who want to stone her. As they approach, Jesus continues to sit and the men ask him for his opinion regarding the teachings written about a woman caught in adultery being stoned to death. What did he say? Jesus replied that he who is without sin should throw the first stone. The men slowly dropped the stones and left. Jesus then asked the woman where her accusers were. She replied they were gone. Jesus said he would not accuse her either and to go and sin no more.

Different Bibles differ as to where this took place. Some say the wall of the city, others say the synagogue. The difference doesn't matter. The important thing is there was a woman, a group of men who wanted to stone her, and there was Jesus. For the purposes of simplicity, I prefer to use the most popular version which is where the woman is chased to the wall.

The woman, accused of adultery, is running towards the wall of the city. Close behind, a mob of men chase her, brandishing stones. It is safe to assume she is scared, probably crying, maybe screaming for mercy, since she surely fears for her life. She probably knows she has no chance of salvation, for those who chase her are on the side of the law of the times, and those that do not join the mob possibly shout encouragement. Perhaps some of the women feel compassion for her but they would assuredly remain quiet. She has sinned and therefore she must pay the price.

The men chasing her have formed a mob. Unless she committed her adultery in the middle of the town square, probably only one or two of the men actually can say they caught her in the act. Even more probable is that only one person in the mob, her husband, actually caught her in the act. The rest of the men obviously are followers, men who heard the accusations of the husband and joined him in his task. Now they chase her to the wall, stones in hand, screaming insults, calling for her punishment, ready to do as they have been taught was right and just. They are following the teachings of their faith of the time. They have no fear of being stopped in their quest of stoning the woman. They have probably worked themselves into a frenzied state not unlike the out-of-control mob scenes we witness on the news today, although on a smaller scale. They are the accusers.

Jesus sits near the wall writing, or drawing in the sand. He surely hears the cries and the screams of the woman as she runs hysterically towards the wall. She probably starts to realize she's at the end of the line. Jesus surely hears the shouts and insults of the men chasing her. As they near the wall, their excitement and mob frenzy surely rises. Yet, even as she reaches the wall and turns, knowing there is no place left to run – even as the men gather near her, picking up stones, shouting insults at her, even as some of them raise their arms ready to release their projectiles; Jesus sits calmly by, writing in the sand and saying nothing. He could have made the men trip and fall, with only a thought, allowing the woman to get away. He could have made the stones so heavy, or so hot, the men would have dropped them to the ground. Jesus could have imposed his will at any instant, yet he didn't, for he knows the heart of man and so loves us that he leaves us free. Jesus is love, justice and forgiveness.

One of the mob, probably the husband or a priest, turns to Jesus. Whether to test Jesus or to reinforce their courage and justification, the man states that it is written that an adulteress should be stoned to death and asks Jesus' opinion on the matter. Jesus remains seated and calm. He replies that he who is without sin should throw the first stone. The mob upon hearing this becomes troubled and men begin to drop their stones to the ground and leave.

One gets the notion from the Bible that the men were probably not too happy about this and left begrudgingly. Chances are some of the members of the mob were disappointed in not being able to quench their thirst and lust for vengeance. Their hysteria calmed and the crowd dispersed. Jesus says no more to them but goes to the woman, who has remained near the wall.

Jesus asks the woman," Where are those that would judge you?"

She replies, "They are gone."

Jesus states, "Then, nor will I judge you. Go and sin no more."

The mob did not judge her. Therefore, Jesus did not judge her. Incredible! Here is a woman, who has lived a whole life of 16, 18, 20 years, the Bible does not say. Maybe she spent most of her life helping others. Maybe she even helped some of the men that were going to stone her. Maybe she was the sole supporter of her parents. Probably, before this incident, she was thought to be a woman of honor or she would have been stoned long before. She was married and this also shows that she was a woman of some honor. Yet, because of one apparent sin, the men of the community were ready to forget her whole life and destroy her. Jesus knew her life. He knew every second of her existence. He did not forget any and all good that this person had done for one downfall. He did not judge her.

How many times have I raised back my rock-filled hand, ready to throw it with all my might? As a truck driver, I spent a few years traveling throughout North America, both in Canada and the USA. During the day I would drive 500 to 600 miles, and then at night I would park in some truck stop or other. My C.B. *(citizen band)* radio was always on as a form of communication, distraction and to receive any valuable information on the road conditions ahead.

If a conversation during the day fell on the subject of prostitutes, those holding the conversation would refer to them as "lot lizards". Then, at night, if their services were desired, the same people would now refer to prostitutes as "commercial company." The stones thrown by day became flowers by night.

Throughout society, people have quickly denounced prostitutes and homosexuals as outcasts. For the most part, they were not allowed in our churches and any person associating with these people, even if only in friendly conversation, were also frowned upon by passersby and by the church. Recently, a confessed homosexual was ordained a minister and this opened up a whole, "can of worms".

Ministers, judges, and other professional people were cast away and lost all including their positions in society, regardless of any previous works, because they were caught in the company of a prostitute. In most cases, the person caught with a prostitute lost all credibility, and in some cases became destitute, despite any and all good that they had previously done. Meanwhile, in some high-profile cases, the prostitute, for her part, gained notoriety and temporary fame while her riches increased. All of this accusing and judging, all of this rock-throwing was done by members of the church and the good Christian society of our times. Naturally, no thought was given to the fact that more than two out of three Christian marriages end up in divorce. Many of our children, by the time they are in sixth grade, are up to their second and third fathers. We have two and three cars in our driveways. We have a television, vcr/dvd, stereo, computer, and machines for playing games in every room of our house, and yet we get upset, look away or even cross the street if a homeless person approaches us for a few pennies. We lift our arms, always ready to throw the stone.

Once, in a place I'll not mention to protect the innocent, I was to receive a load of coffee beans to be delivered to another location. After backing up to the ramp I was informed that workers would come out to load my 53-foot-long trailer. As it happens, two Afro-American young men were put to the task. It was a very hot day. The temperature was in the low 90's.

The young men had to bring pallets stacked with 50-pound bags of coffee beans onto the trailer and then remove the heavy bags of coffee beans from the pallets and place them on the floor of the trailer. It was, to say the least, a hot and tiring job as the temperature inside the trailer was probably over 100 degrees Fahrenheit. I asked if I could assist and was told by one of the young men that it was against company policy and they would get into trouble if I tried to help. I sat to one side and as I watched them work I tried to converse with them, but their responses were short and seemed not too friendly.

Finally, it was time for them to take a break and, as there was a confectionary store just across the street, I asked if I could get them a soft drink. At first, they declined, but I insisted, stating that it was my treat and finally they accepted. Soon, cola in hand, we sat on sacks of coffee beans. They noticed my package of cigarettes and asked what kind they were. I said they were Canadian. I offered them one to try and they accepted. Then they became friendlier and we had an interesting little chat. The young men were inquisitive about the snow in Canada.

While we were talking, a white male stepped out of the office and walked past us. My greeting was ignored and if eyes could kill I would not be here to write this now. The two young men returned to their task, although at a quicker pace and with more conversation, and within an hour I was loaded and ready to leave. I proceeded to the office where the same white gentleman gave me my manifests. Since he seemed not in a good mood I asked if I had done something wrong. He advised me that if the KKK saw me I would find out. He advised me to get in my truck and leave without stopping until I was well away from the area.

Distraught, for I had not even considered such a thing as the KKK, I drove for many hours until I was in the next state before I dared stop. When I stopped for the night I made sure I was in a relatively safe location and my concerns did not leave me until I had crossed the border and was back close to home.

All the threats, anxiety, hatred and fear, and for what? Because I had bought a soft drink and had friendly conversation with two people of a different race? Had I been the same race as them or vice versa, none of these things would have happened. We raise our arms always ready to throw the stones.

When I contemplated all of these things I realized how many times my arm was lifted, holding a big rock, ready to throw it. I realized that I'm still ready to throw the stone today. Then I took a closer look at the stone and on it was written; "hatred, vengeance, deceit, lust, jealousy, self-righteousness, intolerance, --- HYPOCRISY

The lord has blessed me with the knowledge and realization that I am a hypocrite. Will this cause me to stop? I would like to think so, but I doubt it. Will this knowledge cause me to try to stop? I hope so. I know that I'm human; I know that I'm a sinner. I know that God created me. I know that he sent Jesus to save me. I know that Jesus knows me. I know I'm in his hands for I've asked him to put me there and he has promised that if we ask and believe that we have received, then it will be so.

Wealth

I thought of the rich merchant who asked Jesus what he should do to receive the gift of heaven. Jesus replied that he should sell all that he had, give the proceeds to the poor and follow him. The rich merchant turned away, unable to comply and Jesus said to his followers that it was easier for a camel to go through the eye of a needle than it was for a rich man to get into heaven.

I've been taught to give to charities, churches etc. in order to attain heaven. Religious leaders criticize other religions for their different ways of collecting money. Yet all religions I know of collect money in one way or another. When I thought of what happened with the encounter between Jesus and the rich man, I began to wonder if being rich was a grievous sin and heaven was a place only for the poor. Fortunately, I've never been rich.

Is it only those who do not desire heaven that desire riches in this world? Religious leaders have told me that God can act by allowing someone to win a lottery, but it was highly unlikely. All of the religious teachers I have spoken with seem to agree that wealth leads to sin and damnation. Yet most religions are indeed rich. It seems to me that if all of the rich gave all they had to the poor we would be left with a world of poor and no prospect for the future. To give all away and have no long-term means to help doesn't add up to me.

I looked again at the events between the rich man and Jesus. The rich man came up to Jesus and asked what he could do to get into heaven. Jesus told him to sell all that he had and give the proceeds to the poor and follow him (Jesus). The rich man could not leave the security and prestige of his wealth and refused Jesus then turned away and left. On the surface it looks like he was condemned because he was rich and could not give it up. This might be true as far as it goes but I began to question if there was a deeper truth that has nothing, or very little to do with money.

All of Jesus' followers had to give up the lives they were living to follow him. Peter, for instance, gave up his home, his wife and his fishing business to follow Jesus. Levi *(Mathieu)* gave up his extremely profitable business of tax collection, his authority and his very liberal way of living to follow Jesus. To the followers of Christ, wasn't what they gave up every bit as important to them as wealth was to the rich man? What was the rich man's sin? Was it that he wouldn't give up his riches, or was it that he could not put his faith and love in Jesus above all else? Jesus asked the man to sell all, give all to the poor and follow him, but I wonder if that wasn't just a test of faith? Could he not just as easily have asked him to give part of his riches, or offer his son in sacrifice as with Abraham, or perhaps to lead the poor to a richer land as Moses did? Did not Noah look like a fool to his neighbors as he built the arc? Did not all of these great saints put all of their lives and earthly possessions on hold or abandon them totally because they somehow believed in the voice of God and the whisper in their souls?

Our bodies and souls are in constant conflict. Our bodies have needs and wants and in moderation, most of these are not evil, yet when we over-indulge, it becomes bad for both the body and the soul. I have been fortunate enough to have had the teachings, watched the religious movies and read the books of some of the saints of this world. I have visited the places where some of them lived and seen the results of the miracles God did through them. Somehow, I got the impression that these great souls were living without sin. Now, as I think of what I saw and read I believe they were people just like any other person in this world, none of them more or less great. Are we not all saints with some just more active and focused than others? Did not Christ say that if we had faith the size of a mustard seed we could move mountains?

Therein, I expect, is the main difference between most of the world and the great saints. Did the saints know they were sinners, but had so much faith in the love and forgiveness of God that instead of focusing on their sins and weaknesses, they put all else aside to focus on God? Did they only do what they felt inside that they had to do, and rely on a loving and merciful God to work around their humanness? Didn't one of the apostles ask Jesus to show him his sins so that he may live a pure life? Though the apostle was following Jesus and living his life in the presence of Christ, didn't Jesus say to the apostle that his sins were too many and that the apostle would die if all his sins were revealed to him? The Bible tells us the Apostle was torn apart by this revelation but it did not sway him. The Apostle put this aside and continued to follow Jesus and have faith in the love and mercy of God.

This is where I think the rich man failed. He would not put aside the 'God of money' in which he put all of his trust and his security in order to put God first and foremost in his heart. Did he suppose his money would see him comfortably through life and refuse to put that faith in God instead? Do we call on God for help when we have a good job, extra money, lots of food and drink, and all of the diversities we desire? God, I think, would be happy if we prayed once in a while, or thanked him now and then when we are living the good times. If disaster strikes in our lives, all of a sudden we are back to praying, and pleading for God to save us. Such is the normal life of a child. Such it is that we are children of God.

Is wealth just about money or is it anything that we have so much of that we merely indulge and indulge some more with no thought of anything else? Is wealth anything in life that we find so important to us it supercedes all else? Can wealth be a house, a car, a person, a lifestyle? Can sex, booze, gambling, work, leisure etc. all be 'riches'? Can everything also be good? All was created by God and given to mankind whether we think we made it ourselves or not. All can be taken from us by God if he so desires. However, like the rich man, God does not take from us that which he has given; but, asks us to give up that which he knows is not good for us and offers us the things that will lead us to him and the greater glory of heaven. "Sell all that you have and give the proceeds to the poor, then come and follow me".

Love

The first time I heard from others that God is love I tried to imagine God's love in an absolute perfect form. I quickly discovered the task was futile and well beyond my comprehension. The closest I could come is to imagine the person or thing I love most in life and try to magnify my feelings a million-fold. Then I realized even this could not come close to God's perfect love.

Still, using the people I love most, I asked myself if I could sit in front of a big book enumerating to them all of the things they did in their lifetimes that I did not like, or that hurt me? Would they, or could they, or did they ever read from some sort of big book listing all of my faults to me? Thinking these thoughts made me feel bad; I hurt and wanted to cry. I felt sure such an exercise would also make those I love cry and this also hurt me. If these thoughts made me feel this way even while I was alone in my truck, thinking of my imperfect love for the ordinary people in my life then how, I asked myself, could one of perfect and infinite love be sitting in front of a book of my life waiting to condemn me for my faults?

It didn't and doesn't make sense to me that such a love could even think of hurt and pain, and if this is true, then could the opposite be true? What if God is looking through his book of life (Book of Judgment) reading every line, every word, looking for the slightest good I might have done so that I may be allowed into Heaven with him to share in his eternal love?

I envisioned dying and going in front of God, my soul black and dirty from my sins. Kneeling with my head to the floor I'm crying, filled with sorrow for my faults. I cry, "Lord, I am so sorry; I lead a terrible life and do not deserve to enter your kingdom. I am before you begging for mercy, knowing that I deserve only your wrath."

God, in my thoughts, looks down upon me and then at his book and says, "Yes your sins are many, but as I look I see that once you saw my child was hungry and gave him food, My daughter cried and you embraced her and soothed her sorrow. Though your sins are many you gave love to these.

Come and be filled and I'll sooth your sorrow."

When this came to my mind I felt good, like a small child who knows he has done wrong and been chastised, but who, five minutes later, can be found sitting on the lap of the loved one who scolded him, happy and playing. Does 'God is love' mean he wants to hold me in his arms rather than scold me?

Wouldn't it be nice if in our lives we could live like this? What if a man (or woman) after years of marriage came to the other to confess an indiscretion such as having had an affair, and the other partner, though deeply hurt, replied, "You have gravely sinned, but for years you have been faithful. Because of this you are truly forgiven and loved," *(as I wrote in the chapter on prayer, my common-law wife demonstrated such an act of forgiveness towards me and it changed my life and played a major role in my conversion)* I'm not trying to say that forgiveness is easy. It can take some time to reach that point. But is it not through forgiveness that we can find our inner peace?

Now what if this were also true for all of the faults and shortcomings of those we have any kind of relationship with? Would this not be more like love and how one such as God might be in his perfect love? The more I thought about this, the more I realized that God, who is Love, might also be a friend and not the master to be feared that I had always thought him to be. I believe it is at this point that my relationship towards my Lord began to change. It was as if I had taken my first baby step.

If God is love and we are of God, shouldn't it be a lot easier to love than to hate? Sometimes love is painful, yet, when holding and being held by someone you love, or just snuggling on the sofa watching TV, isn't it always a wonderful feeling that makes everything else make sense? What troubles can invade your mind when your baby is on your lap, laughing at your antics?

I began to enjoy God as a friend and confidant with whom I could share my innermost secrets. My joys and fears, my strengths and weaknesses, my accomplishments and defeats could all be laid to rest at his feet. He is always there, completely understanding me and sharing my feelings. I began to understand so many things with regard to what we call religion and my beliefs in God, so much so, that everything changed. God became a friend and no longer a fierce judge, the Bible was no longer a book of rules and regulations but a book of love filled with stories of God's love for us and how we can love each other. My daily life was no longer a question of what did I do wrong today. My stress level dropped tremendously and like a child at play, I have begun to learn how to take things in stride, knowing that God is always there. God has become my greatest comfort. I once heard a saying I now think of when in troubled times, or when I feel unsure as to a decision I should make, or an action or inaction I should take. It is simply this and many of us have heard it said before. *"I do my best and let God do the rest"*.

I came to this conclusion and offer it for your consideration:

If God is love then he must be the noun love. He must be a love so infinitely strong that it has its own form. He must be so pure he cannot harbour any of the anti-love feelings so common to us humans.

We humans are perhaps a part of him, but, we can only be the verb love. *I love you. Do you love me?* We can say *I'm in love* or *I love* or *I don't love.* But we cannot truly say I am love.

If God is love then wouldn't heaven be a place of love? Not the image I've always been given of angels sitting around playing a harp and singing hymns, but a place where all of our interactions with others are filled with pure love. Wouldn't it be a place devoid of hate, jealousy, and mistrust, competition for affection, paranoia, deceit, judgment, or insecurity? All souls would be exactly the same in love. All would be an equal part of God's love.

Could it be that when we die, LOVE is a part of us that remains and lives forever in the realm of Heaven? If so, could it be that choosing love is choosing God and thus is the path to Heaven? Could it really be that simple?

Every day I try to repeat this little prayer, *'Whatever it takes Lord, I want to be yours.'*

Faith

Seven o'clock. The sun is up and it's time to get rolling. I grab a gear and pull my rig out of the parking lot and onto the highway, I have a lot of miles to cover today but that's okay. I turn on the radio and try to find a station to my liking but nothing keeps my attention for very long. Finally, I turn it off and allow my mind to go where it wants. Or perhaps I put in a tape and listen to the Bible for a while.

Soon I am contemplating my faith again and then I begin to think about faith in general. What is faith? It's written all over the place in the Bible. Where does it come from? What does it do? How do I know if I have it and if I don't, how do I get it?

My mind wonders – if one has faith as big as a mustard seed – Ye of little faith – faith, hope and charity. I could look it up in the dictionary or on my computer. I suppose I could ask and at some point, I probably will, but for now I want to know what it means to me and for me. The miles tick off as I continue to contemplate the question, and as I do, a story forms in my mind:

As Jesus and Peter watched from Heaven, a young man sat on the porch of his farmhouse reading the Bible. As he read, he came to where Jesus said that if one had a mustard seed worth of faith he could move a mountain. As it turned out, the man had a hill on his land that made it hard for him to cultivate a fair portion of his field.

"I have faith," the man said. Looking at the hill, he got up and walked to its base. There he held up his hands toward heaven and stated, "I have faith in the Lord; therefore – hill, I order you to move to the side of this property."

The hill didn't move and the man, after three tries, said," I must be doing something wrong for the hill did not move." He then turned from the hill and returned home.

Jesus, with a smile said to Peter, 'There goes a man of little faith, but with a heart to try."

Peter nodded in agreement.

Arriving home, the man returned to his Bible. There he read of prayer and fasting so the next morning he returned to the base of the hill armed with a loaf of bread and some water. Looking toward heaven, he surmised, "I will stay at the base of the mountain for one day and one night of prayer and fasting, and then the Lord will see I have faith and tomorrow when I command the hill to move it will obey."

The next morning, the loaf of bread and his water long gone, tired from not sleeping for 24 hours, he gave praise to the Lord. Turning to face the hill, he then raised his hands toward heaven and commanded the hill to move to the edge of his property. Still the hill did not move, even after three commands to do so. Bewildered, the man returned to his home where he slept for the rest of the day.

Jesus, still smiling, said to Peter, "This man persists but still lacks faith."

Peter, smiling back at Jesus, nodded his agreement.

On the third day, the man once again returned to his Bible to find the answers. He read how God created Heaven and Earth, the stars and the moon, the land and the waters. He read how God created the fish that swim in the sea, the birds that fly in the sky and the animals that roam the land. He learned how God created man and how God put mankind in charge of his garden. Then, turning to the New Testament, he read that if he asked the Lord, believing that he would receive, then it would be so.

Unrelenting, he again went to the hill and fasted and prayed. Then, turning to the hill, he raised his hands toward the sky and beseeched the Lord. "I am but a mortal who has faith in you. I have fasted and prayed. You have put me in charge of your garden. I believe that you will give me what I ask. Then he commanded the hill to move to the edge of his property. Still, the hill remained immobile.

The man looked again to the sky and said, "Lord, you created all that exists. You put this hill where it now sits therefore you must have a good reason for wanting it there. Who am I to question your judgment or try to change what you have done." He then turned and returned home singing praises to the Lord.

Jesus looked at Peter with a huge smile and said, "There goes a man of great faith."

Peter, also jubilant, nodded his agreement.

Unequivocal Love

So is faith to me the knowledge that if I believe enough in God I'll be given all that I want when I want it and think I need it? Or, is true faith the knowledge that God will be there with me to rejoice in the good times and suffer with me in the bad times that must also come; that he will be my strength when I need it most and at my final hour he will be there to bring me to the father? Is it the belief that God gives me what is good for me when I need it even if what I want and what I get are not one and the same? Maybe I don't have to know what faith is as long as I believe that God will give me the faith I need when I need it to continue on toward the fulfillment of his plan for me.

Miracles

The sun rose, the sun set, and mankind called it day. During this day, as in every day throughout the various parts of the world and amongst the different people of the world, everything possible happened as well as some things thought impossible. There was joy and sorrow, happiness and tragedy. Things were destroyed and others built. Some things were found while others were invented. Some things were blended together to make something new and different. Yet not one thing was created on this or any other day by mankind.

We look for miracles and when we find one, we set out to disprove it. We search high and low to find a miracle of God, yet we are blind, for the world is full of miracles that we have become so accustomed to seeing that we are now complacent and treat them as normal.

―――――――――

I was introduced to Brother André at an early age by my mother and my grandmother. The story went that my mother, at the tender age of four, could not walk and could hardly eat. Doctors did all they could but they had advised my grandmother that her daughter would probably never walk.

My grandmother was a very religious person and had heard of the miracle man of Mont Royale in Montreal. One morning she took my mother and went to the basilica and there, with my mother in her arms, my grandmother climbed the stairs leading to the front doors of the oratory on her knees, praying as she went. At the top of the stairs, she met Brother André. He rubbed St. Joseph's oil on my mother's legs and gave a bottle to my grandmother, telling her to massage her with it every day. Sometime later, my grandparents returned to the hospital with my mother. There they placed my mother on the floor and there wasn't a dry eye in the place when my mother ran down the corridor and into the doctor's arms.

Roland R. J. Robert

I don't recall going to visit the oratory myself until I was a young man. But I do remember the arresting effect it had on me to walk into the basilica, but mostly when I entered the tiny church which was the first church built on the mountain. Later when I was living with the religious community, I was given the task of going to the oratory and coming back with a statue of St. Joseph. *(Introducing St. Joseph into the community as the mother superior had put it.)*

I felt close to Brother André and followed with interest as he rose to sainthood. I purchased the movie version of his life's story and watched it more than once.

Then, one day in 2008, tragedy struck when my closest friend announced he had lung cancer. It was as if my life was ending. To me, he was more than a friend; he was like a brother. We were always together, working around the park where we lived.

I began to get a strong urge – almost like a calling – to go to the oratory in Montreal to get some of St. Joseph's oil. I couldn't shake it, and remembering the story of my mother, it didn't take much convincing. One Sunday morning, I was off to visit Brother André.

When I got to the Oratory I climbed one flight of stairs on my knees while stopping on each step to pray for my friend. Then I would stand for a flight of stairs, again stopping on each step to pray. I continued to repeat this until I reached the top of the long staircase. Inside the church, I prayed at the tomb of Brother André and then purchased a bust of the good brother and some of the St. Joseph's oil, had it blessed and returned home.

The priest who introduced the tradition of the rubbing of St. Joseph's oil to Brother André is said to have advised the good brother that if the oil didn't heal the body it was good for the soul. Such was the case for my friend. His body did not heal and he passed away two years later.

On the very day I brought him the oil he couldn't get over the fact that someone could do such a thing for him. After I showed him what to do with the oil, he immediately changed and became a religious man, openly praying and asking God to bless those he met. He shared his oil with another person we knew who had cancer until I had to return to get them some more.

After his passing, I went through a troubled time. I stopped going to church and didn't pray much. This went on for a couple of years until one Sunday morning when I was on my way to get groceries. The road I took went by the church I had attended and I began to feel an urge to go to mass. The clock on my car radio said mass was about to start. I decided not to go but the closer I got, the stronger the feeling got until finally I pulled into the parking lot, called my wife, and advised her that I was going to church and would do the groceries later. As I walked into the church, I was blown away. There at the foot of the altar stood a large portrait of Brother André surrounded by flowers. It was the day they were celebrating his ascension to sainthood.

From that day forward, I returned to church on a regular basis. About a year later, my wife and I moved from the park where we lived and now live a nice quiet life in the country. I go to church regularly, have published my first book and am writing this one. I have a small shrine in my office devoted to Jesus and Mary. I have there a picture of Mary Magdalene and a small statue of Brother André.

I returned to see the good brother not long ago because doctors discovered lumps on my stepdaughter's breast. While I was there, I recalled a story I read of a man who, after being healed, began to drive people on a pilgrimage to another such basilica on a regular basis. I began to get the urge to do the same for the St. Joseph's Oratory and it stayed with me.

My son was supposed to come with me that Sunday but had to cancel. Later that week, I had occasion to speak of the trip with his wife and she stated she would also like to go, so a trip was scheduled with my son, his wife, and two daughters for the summer. The following Sunday, I spoke to a couple of friends after mass to give them a couple of articles that I had promised them. We were supposed to have met the Sunday before so when I apologized for not showing up and explained why, the lady immediately said she hadn't been there since her childhood and would like to go again someday. She and her husband had no means of travel so I said I would take them when I returned. Lately, when I look at the shrine in my room, I am reminded that it is missing the statue of St. Joseph.

I guess another trip to the Oratory is coming due.

Me and Judas

I was involved in a court case that dragged on for over two years. One day I received a telephone call from my lawyer stating that the other party refused the latest offer and did not want to make a counter-offer. I told him I was preparing an offer and would forward it. He told me he would look at it and call me back on Friday.

Friday came and went without a word from him. A week later, I still had not heard anything except I received a notice from the court that the hearing had been rescheduled for November 30. Frustrated by the apparent inactivity and not knowing what was going on, I decided to call my lawyer to see what was happening and try to entice a response.

As I prepared for my day, and before I made a telephone call, I decided I would ask for guidance from my daily reading of the Bible. Immediately, in my mind I began thinking of Judas and his betrayal of Jesus. I remembered I had heard Judas was convinced that by having him brought before the courts, Jesus would be put in a position to reveal himself and would have to act to show the world he was the Messiah.

No one can get into the mind of Judas. I've also heard he was a thief and was only interested in money. He apparently belonged to a group of activists which was growing impatient with the way Jesus was acting.

Was Judas impatient? Was he frustrated? Did he lack in faith? Did he believe by forcing the issue and selling Jesus out that he was actually helping Jesus complete his mission? Did he help Jesus complete his mission of redemption?

A few minutes later, I was ready to read from the Bible and when I opened it, I fell upon the part where Jesus sent the disciples into the towns and villages to prepare the way for him.

So often I find it hard to 'go with the flow'. Was I frustrated like Judas might have been? Was I impatient like Judas probably was? Did I lack in my faith like Judas did? Was I failing in my trust in God? My answer to these questions is definitely Yes, Yes, and Yes again. May God forgive me my shortcomings. I decided not to call my lawyer.

How many times in life do I get impatient, like I want to pull the rip cord before jumpiing out of the plane? Isn't that what credit cards are all about? *I want it. I can't afford it. I got it. Jesus came to save us. He's not doing it. He'll have to do it now.*

Extremist is just another word for impatient when one really looks at it. Extremists can't get what they want. They can't get it now so they take radical action, something akin to a temper tantrum. Sometimes this type of action can be justified and sometimes it can't. But at all times one must be careful not to be a Judas.

I confess I am one of the guiltiest. I've had maxed out credit cards, because when I wanted something, I **needed** it now. The result is what God provides for me to look after my family is squandered on paying off debts I should not have. Where would God have taken me in life had I not spent my life so callously? By choosing my way, I have lost God's way. But God did not abandon me and has chosen for me a new way if I wish to follow it. Or like Judas, I can abandon God to self-destruction – but God will never abandon me.

The Passion of Christ

Jesus Christ Superstar, Jesus of Nazareth, The Passion; these movies were all criticized by different religious organizations. Some church leaders advised their parishioners not to watch them because the theatrics were accused of bordering on sacrilege and heresy.

The Passion was criticized for the graphic depiction of the crucifixion of Jesus. Earlier movies were scorned because no actor was worthy of portraying Jesus. How my father's generation got upset when Jesus was called a Superstar.

I read the Bible and watched the movies and listened to the church leaders but still there seems to be a void, something missing, unseen. The same old worn out question keeps returning, "What makes the suffering of Jesus, as cruel as it was, any different or worse than that of others who suffered great atrocities by their enemies. The great martyrs themselves sometimes suffered hours and days of excruciating torture before they were permitted to die. What made Jesus different from them and them from Jesus?" When I contemplate this, one thing keeps coming to my mind. What if we're not seeing the whole picture surrounding the passion of Christ?

If God is love, then Jesus, the son of God, conceived of the Holy Spirit, must also be love. What if Jesus came to earth, not to die but to teach us of the love of his father? What earthly father sends his son or daughter off to war to die? Do we not watch them go, proud that they are doing their duty, fighting to free the oppressed with the hope the message will be received and they will return safely when the war ends? Unfortunately many have died and more will die in conflict. How many wars have to be fought before we understand that we do not send our youth out to die, but to live so that many more can live free to love?

Jesus came to us and spoke only of love and the love God has for us. Could we not have heeded the message without Jesus having to die? Thousands followed him and heard his message. Countless were healed physically and emotionally by him. He raised the dead and chased evil from the obsessed. He did all he could to get us to change our ways and learn to love as God loves us. Still, we didn't listen. One week before he was crucified he entered Jerusalem and the crowds hailed him and laid palms across the path before him as he rode through the gates on a mule. Who stood back and cast a watchful eye on the proceedings scrutinizing his every movement? The Romans watched to insure there would be no public unrest or rioting, just as police watch demonstrators today. As the police do today, the Romans had probably already gathered a lot of intelligence about this popular Rabbi and decided he was harmless to the Roman agenda; otherwise wouldn't they have arrested Jesus before this?

The high priests and the scribes scrutinized Jesus with a critical eye. Were they jealous? Did the high priests of those days not live as the leaders of our day? Some were probably jealous, and some were probably afraid for their status in life. Some possibly were curious and some might have begun to believe in Jesus as the Messiah. The little I see in the Bible tells me that for sure, their world was being disrupted. For the most part, it appears the priests only wanted to protect their way of life, their religious beliefs and the people for whom they felt responsible, while not upsetting the Romans. Although the Romans allowed the Jewish people to practice their faith, the high priests knew if there was unrest, the privilege could be taken away from them. However, Jesus was causing unrest; therefore they used an interpretation of the rules of their faith to put Jesus to death.

Another aspect was that the high priests of the day lived like kings. They were highly respected and obeyed by the community. Next to the king and the Romans they probably had the most power and probably used that power to manipulate the other two whenever possible. Jesus comes along and preaches against them, breaks down their laws and their rules, and tries to make them understand religion is made for man and not the other way around. He upsets the highest of the hierarchy of priests.

I would suggest that the death of Jesus is political, but even this is not clear. He is ordered to be flogged but the Roman soldiers overdo it. No one orders the crowning of thorns or the red horse blanket over the wounds. The covering of his head and the punching was not ordained, nor was the ripping off of his beard. The crowds turning on him as he was marched to Mount Calvary throwing stones, spitting, punching, kicking, none of this was ordained. The Bible implies that even some of the Romans had pity on him. The Jewish people, God's chosen people, had turned on him.

What some have suggested and what I now bring forward is that this is the one time in history where Heaven and Hell came together to fulfill God's plan. What we know as the Devil and Hell threw all they had at Jesus. *(We only see the physical part of this battle)* If Jesus had faltered for one second; had he for a moment wished vengeance or felt hate, denounced the Father, etc., the world as we know it probably would have ended. Jesus was tortured, not by man, but by the evil within the human race and all of the accumulated evil of mankind through the centuries from the beginning to the end. This could be why we are also responsible for his crucifixion.

Christ Crucified

I go to church and see the cross at the head of the chapel. In modern years, a number of Catholic churches expose different statues of Christ resuscitated or no statue at all on the cross. When I was young, most crucifixes showed a statue of Christ nailed to the cross with the crown of thorns, and leaning forward in death. To me, when I gaze upon the cross and see the crucified Christ, it reminds me of how much he suffered so I might be saved. It also reminds me of those whom I've heard say things like; *If God let his son suffer and be tortured like this, he must be a sadist;* or *if God were human he'd be charged with criminal neglect; how can a father let his son suffer like that?* And it goes on and on.

I don't understand this logic. I sometimes wonder if we're not, 'passing the proverbial buck'. Did God let this happen to his son or did we do it to his son? The same people, who accuse God, do so at the very moment they stand at the airport, train station or shipyard to say good bye to their sons and daughters as they send them off to war. Do they send them to be shot, or stabbed, or blown up, or torn apart by shrapnel? Should the parents of every soldier who is killed or maimed be charged with criminal neglect? When our sons and daughters die at war or otherwise trying to save others, don't we make heroes of them?

Which house has lost a child and does not hold dear pictures and other replicas to honor that child? State monuments are raised in their names with a replica picture or statue and a plaque to state the heroic deed they performed to save their friends. Movies are made relating their heroic gestures, regardless of the amount of violence involved. Since the First World War, actual battles have been captured on camera and shown, in all their gory detail, in movie theatres, and now on TV and the internet. Are we all sadists?

Even as I sit and write this, in the other room, I hear a reality program playing on TV describing a murder-rape crime in explicit detail to all who are watching. It's hard to find a station today that is not showing such crimes in explicit detail seemingly making it easy for someone else to commit the same crime. Our kids are playing video games, shooting and killing, blowing up and destroying property, with high-quality graphics that make the images appear real. This, our children do for hours a day. Where are our children? Drive around any neighborhood and the streets, yards and school grounds *(when school is out)* are bare. Are parents today negligent?

When I was young, parents were responsible for the actions of their children, but at that time, just one parent had to work, usually there was one TV per household. There were a lot less vehicles on the road and getting around was harder than today. It was much easier to spot any vehicle that didn't belong in the community and neighborhood watch was just the natural thing to do. Our children were safer and less influenced by the outside world back then. Most media were less interested in their legal rights to show and tell and more committed to their moral obligations as to how much they should show and tell.

We are responsible for all of this. We caused the world that we now live in to happen. Yet we had and still have the power to stop it, but we don't. Why? As far as I can see, these changes have happened mostly in the name of freedom.

'Why did God allow this to happen?' What an overworked cliché that statement is. What did we do to stop whatever we're blaming on God? I don't believe for one moment God sent his son Jesus to earth to be tortured, crucified and killed. First of all, Christ's death wasn't final. Christ is alive now, and forever, and we are saved. All we need to do is accept it. Were we not given every opportunity not to crucify him?

Reading the passion of Christ, I see many chances given us to save him. All we had to do was embrace his teachings. It wasn't necessary for Judas to turn him in. There was no need for the religious leaders of the day to be jealous of him, or to feel threatened by him, and the crowd didn't have to call out for Barabbas to be saved on that fateful day. Who forced anyone to spit on him or throw rocks at him and blaspheme him on the march to his death?

It seems to me instead of finding ways to blame God we should be forever grateful he did not choose to seek revenge on us for what WE did. We should forever give praise and thanks for God's eternal love and forgiveness. He, even after all of our transgressions, gave us his son Jesus to be our savior and advocate before God and winning for us that which we do not deserve for ourselves – the gift of eternal life.

Christianity

Now and then

Sunday morning at the end of mass, our parish priest announced the Christmas schedule for religious service. At the end he stated there would be a midnight mass on Christmas Eve. Then he added "If there were people in attendance."

Later that day, as usual, I went to my computer and checked my e-mails. There were the usual jokes and spiritual 'pass it on' messages. Letters of complaint about what non-Christian religions were doing and how they were undermining our Christianity, and some unrelated publicity.

One caught my attention by comparing immigrants of 1911 to today's immigrants. It spoke of how the newcomers to Canada respected and adopted our customs and languages, respected our Christianity, waved our flag and fought with us as Canadians – back then. I couldn't help but ponder all of the changes in the last century.

When emigrants arrived in Canada 100 years ago they didn't have all the social benefits, but neither did Canadians. What they did have was mostly Christian people helping whoever and whenever they could, sometimes with money but usually with sharing and Christian charity as it was meant to be. In 1911, most people remembered and still lived the hardships of their forefathers. The difference was they didn't blame God for their troubles but instead praised him for his daily blessing. 'Our daily bread' did not include money, electronics, a new car etc. Except for the privileged few, Canadians worked from sunrise till past sunset to win what little they had. (There were no unions and labour laws back then) Immigrants didn't receive welfare, but neither did any other Canadian.

Christians, Jews, Muslims, Buddhists, even atheists practiced their beliefs according to their faith. No one worked on Sunday for it was a day of rest; a day when family and friends could get together and strengthen their social bonds. Churches were full on Sunday morning and people who didn't go were shunned. During the month of December, Christmas trees appeared and everywhere one could see manger scenes. Some were store bought but most were handmade. Midnight mass was celebrated at midnight and the churches of all Christian denominations were packed to the point of not even having standing-room. When I look at the remaining churches of that era, they are all big stone cathedrals capable of seating many more of the faithful than today's churches.

The morning of Christmas Day, the father and mother, after being awakened early by the children, went before the Christmas tree, which almost always displayed a manger scene, and the gifts were handed out. Then later in the afternoon, the whole extended family gathered for Christmas dinner and celebrated together until late Christmas night.

———

The song, 'Easter Parade' was not imaginary. There were parades at Easter to celebrate the resurrection of Christ, our Savior. Mostly, they were not commercial parades; they were religious parades led by church leaders and followed by Sunday mass. Immigrants who arrived in our country saw an active Christian community and many were converted. I know this because even as a child and until the later 50s and early 60s, it was so.

So I ask myself, "What do immigrants and non-Christian religions relate to today when they think of Christianity?" Removing Christmas trees from public places? Do today's Christmas trees reflect the birth of Christ, or the presents under them? Actually, isn't the tree just a symbol of a holiday unless we adorn it with angels, and the manger scene? I wonder is it only Christians that put up a tree and other ornaments for the holiday?

Do we praise the birth of Jesus, or max out our credit cards competing to purchase the most impressive presents? Why do the spiritual leaders of our communities have to mention there will be mass only if there is attendance? I would suggest that these are not entirely accurate questions. Although many do spend a lot of money at Christmas-time, it's not only the Christians that do so and the reasons for the spending and purchasing of gifts is as numerous as there are people. I would suggest that people in general, and of all denominations celebrate in the way that suits them, their families and their faiths the best. Although the times have changed, have the hearts of God's children also changed?

Removing the crucifix from schools and public places? Did we even know they were there before we ordered them removed? Perhaps I didn't notice, but I don't remember the last time I saw a crucifix or a religious statue in a Christian home. Do you have one in yours? The crucifix is probably the most prominent symbol in the Christian faith, yet are we really supposed to impose it on others? As Christians, do we not carry the crucifix in our minds and in our hearts? Do not all Christians know of the crucifixion of our lord Jesus Christ? I suggest that the removal of these artifacts from public places might be a Christian way of welcoming those of all faiths into our communities and our lives. Who knows? Perhaps our kind understanding will serve God's purpose to convert others. We should never forget that Jesus wants to bring us to the father.

Some say that we can't pray in school. We can pray whenever and wherever we want too. We just have to pray to ourselves. Internal devotion is the one thing no one can take from us as long as we live.

God gave us a wonderful land where we can practice our faith without persecution and we rewarded him by not practicing our faith but instead we boast of our freedom to do what we wish with our bodies and our lives.

Are we saved because we are Christians or because of our faith in, and our love for God? Do we truly believe we will be saved because we are, 'non practising Christians'?

Why do we so easily believe the prophesies of Nostradamus and others like him to the point of changing what he said so that it will be true? Why do we believe fortune-tellers, clairvoyants and those who try to frighten us with predictions of disasters and the end of the world? Why do we believe those who preach to us only of 'Revelations' and repentance and the fires of Hell without ever speaking of love and forgiveness and the kindness and goodness of God? All of these we so readily seek and believe to hold the answers.

Why do we have so much trouble reading and believing and living by the spirit and meaning of the book God gave us – The Bible?

And who am I to write all this? I am the Christian and I am the Atheist. I am the Jew and I am the Muslim. I am the Buddhist and I am the one who seeks my creator and my salvation. I am you, and you are me, for we are one in this quest for life.

Religious Social Club

I drive down the road feeling disturbed. Earlier, I sat at the truck stop drinking my morning coffee and listening to the newscast on the television above the counter. One of the stories was of a man standing in front of a church holding a baby in his arms. He wanted to have the baby baptized but because he was not a practising Christian, the church leaders refused to baptize the baby. Some of the faithful leaving the church after Sunday service were interviewed by a reporter and most agreed with the clergy. One person stated the church was like a form of social club and if one wanted to be a member, one had to abide by the rules. Is this what our religious beliefs have come to, I ask myself as I continue to drive towards my next delivery; did Jesus die on the cross so we could have a bunch of self-righteous social clubs?

Is the goal of each religion to spend much of its time bringing down the other faiths? Has religion become just some big industrial social club?

Why do we insist on believing our religious leaders must be perfect little gods? Why is it, just because they have chosen to dedicate their lives to preach the word of God that we expect them to be able to 'walk on water'? No matter how much good they've done over the past 20 years, is it right that we should turn from them and destroy their lives just because we found out they are human? Sometimes it appears to me that when it comes to religion and religious leaders we're more prone to witch hunting than to faith, hope and charity.

So should we just forgive and ignore any wrongs committed by religious leaders? I don't believe that forgiveness works that way. If someone punches me in the head, I don't forgive them by just standing there and letting them continue to punch me. If I catch someone stealing from me, I don't think charity demands that I give him what he stole and invite the person to take the rest of what I have. By the same token, when someone does something wrong to me should I mercilessly destroy that person, all of his family, and all of the good things they might have done in the past? Why does the old cliché, 'you're only as good as your last gig' have to be so true in our judgment of people, especially our religious leaders? Is this the rule we would want God to judge us by?

When I was but a teenager, there was a young lady I really cared for. We became close friends. To me, our relationship was like that of brother and sister. Inside, I cared more for her than that but I couldn't express my feelings for there was an enormous barrier standing between us that could not be broken at the time. She was Protestant and I was Catholic.

Society at that time didn't mind friendship between religions but serious relations and marriage were strictly taboo. How you would raise your children was a common argument against mixing religion and relationship. A protestant couldn't go into a Catholic church and of course no Catholic could enter a Protestant church. Where would we get married? If a Catholic married other than in the Catholic church, the marriage didn't count and the person in question was living in sin and would continue to do so until they married in the Catholic church. I believe the opposite was also true. Interdenominational marriages were not permitted in the Catholic Church so such marriages were performed usually by a justice of the peace.

What purpose did this serve? In my case, as with many others, I folded to peer pressure and never revealed my feelings to *(or for)* the young Protestant lady I so cared for. One of the saddest days of my young life was when a few years later, I received an invitation to her wedding. Some 40 years later, I've been married three times and divorced twice. Ten years ago I met and married a wonderful lady and have finally found true happiness in my life. I'm still a Catholic and my wife is Protestant. *(Not the girl of my youth)*

My faith remains the same. I believe in God the Father, the Son and the Holy Spirit. I attend mass almost every Sunday. The most important part of my faith is to receive Holy Communion. All else is important but secondary. So how is that different from any other Christian religion? Why can't I receive communion in any Christian church that offers it? Why can't my children be baptized regardless of what I believe?

Why can't church leaders be permitted to be human?

Idolatry

I look out my window and I see the statue of liberty. In the meantime, I hear someone on my CB preaching that Catholics are idol-worshipers because they have statues of Jesus, Mary and the Saints in their churches and their homes. I visit the Lincoln Monument and think how Catholic shrines are accused of being places housing idols. I wonder if the four figureheads carved on the mountainside at great expense, to be seen for miles around, would be idols if instead they were replaced by the images of Jesus, Mary, and Joseph.

When one has a picture of a loved one in his or her wallet or on a desk, is this an idol that they worship or an image made to represent the ones they love? If one kisses the image, are they practicing idolatry or momentarily feeling closer to their loved ones? Suppose one kneels before the image of their family while away on a long trip and prays to God to keep them safe while they are away. Is this idolatry?

When one wears a cross or other religious piece of jewelry, such as an image of God on their person, is this Idolatry? What about when one wears a wedding ring? What makes that different?

My understanding of Idolatry is that it means worshipping gods other than the one God. (Thor, Zeus, the sun etc.) Statues of these false gods were taken down and many were destroyed. This led us to believe that the statues were idols. These statues only represented the god whose image they were meant to reflect. People of the time prayed to their gods through the image. They did not actually adore the image. We know today that the gods did not exist; therefore the people's prayers were unheard and unanswered.

I would suggest that as we have statues and plaques throughout the world to represent great people who have done heroic deeds so do we have statues of the crucifix, Mary, Joseph and the Saints to remind us of the great deeds of the Christian world. Many, if not most people, pray to their departed ancestors, (mothers, fathers, etc.) for help. How many go to those who claim to be able to speak with the dead? Yet if one claims to pray to Mary or Joseph, asking them to speak to Jesus on their behalf they are accused of Idolatry.

In today's world I would suggest we look more towards our possessions if we want to find idols. The biggest one being money. What would we do if Jesus came to us and said *"Give all that you have to the poor and follow me."?*

Sex and Homosexuality

As I write this, the big issue of the day is homosexuality. Part of the world has come to terms with its existence and the other has not. In today's world, many places allow same-sex marriages, but nonetheless, homosexuality is still a big issue in most places. One state approved and then rejected the law. In the meantime, many same-sex marriages took place. Those who got married by the state are now being told the marriage is not valid. Can we get any crueler to these people?

Are we so obsessed with the few words in the Bible stating that God loathes homosexuals that we forget our Christian values? What happened to love and charity? These two acts which are repeatedly spoken of, and required of Christians throughout the Bible? Not to mention non-judgment - lest ye be judged.

How can God, who is love, loathe anything or anybody the way we take the phrase to describe how he feels about homosexuality? Cannot heterosexuals live in sin and perform acts distasteful to God? If our religious leaders are caught performing homosexual acts, how is that different then when they perform heterosexual acts with prostitutes or cheat on their wives etc.?

When in the Bible we see words such as God hates, or God loathes etc., I do not believe it is meant in the way we feel these emotions. If God is perfect love, he cannot feel any part of anti-love any more than the anti-love can feel any part of love. What's more, I believe that in God's terminology, it would simply be referred to like a magnet when one tries to put the two positive sides or the two negative sides together. It is a term of incompatibility. In the case of the magnet, it's not the magnet that is incompatible but the way it is being used. Turn it so that it is used in a correct manner and it is totally compatible.

There are many ways of experiencing heterosexuality. The most common is the union between a man and women who live together, and enjoy their sexuality as an extension of their love. This, I believe, is what God meant for humankind.

Then there are all of the other ways. These are the ways that displease God. We could also say that God hates or God loathes. Why? Because there is no real love involved and our bodies which house and are temples of our souls are not being used as intended.

Homosexual couples, when permitted by man, can live long, healthy lives together just as heterosexual couples do when a man and a woman are in love with each other. In this case, I believe their sexuality is a part of that love and I suggest that both heterosexuality and homosexuality are compatible with God's love.

Sex for the sake of sex runs rampant today as it did in the time of our Lord Jesus.

Homosexuality was a popular form of entertainment. Men used their slaves in this fashion; soldiers had no problem performing acts with each other. *(I believe it is at the battle of Jericho that God forbids those who had sex the night before to partake in the battle)* All of these acts were committed without the love and commitment that is part of God's love and is therefore incompatible.

Is it for us to say if a relationship, be it heterosexual or homosexual is wrong or are we throwing *(prejudice)* stones?

What is Forgiveness?

Is it to walk up to someone I have wronged and ask for forgiveness? Is it saying, 'I forgive you' to someone who has wronged me? I expect this is a good action when and where possible, but only if it is sincere. But can we only forgive or be forgiven if we can reconciliate with the other person or persons involved?

'Please forgive me' or 'I forgive you' are just words that can mean a lot or nothing at all. God knows what is real and what is not. What if true and complete forgiveness is also manifested by abstinence of action? The absence of hate, jealousy, and vanity; the lack of desire for vengeance etc.. Are these not acts of forgiveness? If I can tear myself away from these negative desires, am I not left with at least the beginning of true forgiveness and love?

There is no past, for if there was then I could go there. I live in the present. I dream and plan for the future and strive to achieve my goals. Some I attain and some I don't. The only thing I can do about the past is remember the good things, but mostly I regret the bad. I cannot change or undo the past. The things I did to others and what others have done to me are over. I can hate and wish harm to those who offended me, but the only thing this could accomplish is hurt to myself. Why live in anguish over what has happened? I would offer that, although I say I have forgiven, my actions might bear witness to the opposite.

What happens when one doesn't forgive even if they believe they have? When one goes near where the other party lives or works, they get an uncomfortable feeling in the pit of their stomach. They will avoid places the other might frequent or they will be on the lookout for the other when in the area. Are there places you go where you hope you won't run into someone? Are there places you avoid in case you might run into that someone? Should you see them would you do anything to avoid them? Would they play on your mind for the rest of the day?

In the meantime, perhaps the other person has forgiven you so they go about their daily routine without giving thought of where they go. Thoughts of seeing you or not don't enter their mind. Should they see you they would nod and carry on their day. The past would be where the past should be and although they might say they haven't forgiven you, their actions would say otherwise.

It is said we should love one another as God has loved us. Is forgiveness not a part of that love? If forgiveness is a part of love and God is love then is not forgiveness one with God? When we ask God for forgiveness he loves and forgives us so as to have no memory of the transgression. God, I would offer, requires no more of us than we can take. Especially: I believe through his mercy, God helps us to find forgiveness if we truly ask it of him.

Abortion

If one would suppose that I should use this as a platform to protest against abortion in the usual sense they would be mistaken. There are many reasons for termination of pregnancy and one could only argue the issue fairly one case at a time. On the other hand, if one were to suppose I should use this forum to lecture for the right of termination I would give the same argument. Neither is it mine to argue nor do I intend to.

The word abortion means termination and each year, countless numbers of children have their young lives terminated by war, famine, disease, neglect, homicide, accident and the list goes on and on. It is for all of these children that I pray and ask for assistance in remembering. A few years ago, a small prayer came to my mind as I sat in a chapel and I have been saying it every time I pray. I look now for help, or perhaps it is the children that look for help in this prayer:

Lord, permit that I spiritually adopt all of the children
Whose lives have been terminated today.
Let me name them life, love, charity.
Let me place them on your sacred altar
Baptize them through your
Sacred Heart and your Precious Blood
So they may receive with us
The Communion of the Saints
And life ever after. – Amen

Body and Soul

There are those who believe evil is transferred through the blood and so refuse to receive blood transfusions for themselves or their families. Many children have died because of this. I have to ask why evil needs such a vessel to transport from one to another body. How did evil enter the first body before transfusion?

Some things definitely can be transmitted through the blood, but these are viruses and diseases that remain in the blood and if not checked can be transferred. Simple medical tests of the blood can discover and eliminate these viruses and make the blood clean, or the blood can be simply discarded and not used. These are not spiritual issues but scientific facts. I have never heard of anyone preaching that God will not allow a soul into heaven because the body was plagued with disease. If one receives blood from a donor who cannot walk, does the recipient also become unable to walk? Or if one receives blood from someone who cannot see, does the recipient also become blind? When Jesus says to go forth and heal the sick and chase away evil spirits, does he mean that evil and sickness are one, or are these two different afflictions the faithful must deal with?

The body, it seems, is nothing more than an ultra-modern vehicle of transportation, not unlike a car, train, boat or plane. As technology advances so do our vehicles, homes, workplaces, articles of amusement and articles of war. Most people own some sort of mechanical mode of transportation such as a car. For those who have lots of money, there are new expensive models of vehicles, but they still break down from time to time and they still grow older. When that happens, one brings the car to the garage where mechanics remove the old broken parts and replace them with new working parts. Satisfied, the customer drives away and continues their business.

Someone with less money will buy an older used car and when it breaks they will go to a big-box store or a used parts store and sometimes they will replace the broken part with one that was stripped from a scrapped car. If one drives a

'Ford' product and replaces a broken part with one that was made for a 'G.M.' does the Ford become a G.M. or does a Toyota become a Honda or a Nissan?

As civilization advances, more is learned about the human body. When I had a kidney removed in my youth I was informed that if the infection had happened 10 years earlier, I would have died because the technology and medical knowledge required to safely remove a kidney did not exist then. Today, we can routinely remove and transplant a kidney. But does that change the person with the new kidney in any way besides enabling them to live a healthier normal life?

For centuries, we have said that love comes from the heart. It might just be the most overused cliché in history. Today, we can fix a heart that is physically broken: replace a dysfunctional heart with a donated heart or a mechanical one. Just like an old car, the heart has to be compatible with the new vehicle it is being installed into or it will not function. So if I were to have a heart transplant would I wake up a changed man, loving the donor's wife and children and forgetting my own? Would I love the people he loved and hate the ones he hated even if I didn't know them before the transplant? Would a heterosexual wake up loving people of the same sex and a homosexual loving those of the opposite sex? I have never heard of any of these things happening.

The only comments I have ever heard is that the person receiving the transplanted heart either didn't survive or they did survive and were granted a few more years on this earth with their families and friends. It appears to me, for those who do not believe in life after death, this should be good news. One has a chance of not extinguishing quite as quickly.

For those, like me, who do believe in God and life after death, perhaps science and technology is a blessing. I have heard comments such as 'God is the only one who should decide life and death.' Or 'When your time comes, there's nothing you can do about it. Science and technology should not interfere.' Hey, who am I to say this train of thought is right or wrong. But here's another suggestion 'If God didn't want us to discover how to help each other in the name of love, then why did he make us with so many interchangeable parts? If one wants to believe evil had a hand in this, that's fine, but I do not subscribe to the thought that evil *(or the devil)* had any part in our creation. Nor do I believe that evil can do anything good such as improve our health or our physical condition of life. My faith is with a loving God who created us in his likeness. *(Our soul)* Does the Bible not say that we are grafted from God's chosen people?

For as many millions of people as there are on this earth there are as many different ideas about religious perception and so I do not profess to have answers, only questions and, at times, perhaps opinions pertaining to my reflections on topics of faith and religion for consideration. I believe that we are each two people: the body and the soul. The Body could, as I have attempted to demonstrate, be as a form of mechanical device created by God to house who we are in his likeness, our soul.

Evil can only attack the body like rust attacks a car. When evil attacks us, if we do not look after it, the rust will spread until it is out of control and we are lost. Rust cannot attack the person or people sitting in the car but only the car in which the people are seated. If the person who owns the car looks after it and has the bodywork done to remove the rust, the vehicle will remain in good shape and be a good vessel of transportation as the person goes about his daily life. If the person does not remove the rust from his vehicle, then the vehicles will be overcome and be no longer serviceable. The ill-maintained vehicle will break down in the desert sun, leaving its occupant (the soul) to slowly perish.

Tranquility

It was a clear night. The full moon sat off in the distance just above the tree line so that it looked like a big yellow ball resting on the uppermost branches of a large pine tree. The November wind howled as it blew across the yard, doing its job cleaning the tree branches of the remainder of their multi-colored leaves. In the darkness, I could see the shadow of the leaves as the wind carried them swirling and twirling until finally, free of the wind's clutches, they fluttered to their resting place on the ground below.

Inside, the wood crackled in the fireplace as flames pranced around the newly-installed log like so many ballerinas dancing in a theatre. Besides the two night-lights, the only other light came from the muted television, where my favorite hockey team had just scored another goal. But my mood was too peaceful for me to become excited about it. Instead I sat in the semi-darkness, my gaze divided between the silent images of the game and the frolicking fingers of flame.

Guilty of getting a little too comfortable, my wife had drifted off to sleep in her recliner chair. For a while, I sat and gazed at the gentle features of her face reflected in the soft glow of the firelight and observed the rhythmic breathing of her peaceful slumber. Soon, she half opened her drowsy eyes and asked in a somnolent whisper, "Why are you looking at me like that?"

Actually, I had been staring in awe and silently thanking God for granting me such a wonderful gift of this marvelous person, his daughter, to share whatever part of my life that he would allow. As I looked into her eyes I simply replied, "Because you're beautiful and I love you."

At 61, she still blushes every time I say she's lovely and smiles the innocent smile of a child as she shyly lowers her eyes. Her only comment was, "You're silly. I love you, too." Then she worked her way out of her chair, gave me a kiss and slowly made her way off to bed with our dog, Angel, in hot pursuit. The cat, sleeping comfortably on the floor near the warm fire looked up but seeing no reason to be disturbed, promptly closed its eyes and went back to sleep. I smiled and continued to enjoy the serenity of the night.

But it wasn't always like this. I remember the putrid stench of my own spiritual death: I remember the hollow emptiness of the ever-present loneliness only temporarily dulled by the entwining of another forlorn body whose name never mattered. No amount of bathing could wash away the filth of my ignominy. No amount of lies could quench the cravings of my conscience and my soul. I was afraid of the dark then, for when I was alone, surrounded by the shadows of obscurity, I could not hide the truth that dwelled within. I was not meant for one-night stands.

I could take no more as I drove home one day after another unrewarding encounter. I screamed at God as tears rolled down my cheeks and I hammered my fist on the steering wheel as I begged for changes in my life. Physically and emotionally drained, I pleaded for God's mercy.

God, in his infinite love of his children, answered my pleas. Within moments of my exiting the shower a friend *(whom I had not heard from in months)* called me on the telephone to ask if I would like to attend a weekend charismatic conference. Without hesitation, I said yes to her and to God. That Friday I drove her to the "Centre D'Amour" in Plantagenet.

During lunch on the second day *(Saturday)* I overheard the people sitting next to me speak of a small cottage that was for rent. It was situated in the campgrounds across the street, which also belonged to the Centre. By the time the lunch period was over, I had visited the cottage and agreed to rent it. And so within two weeks of pleading for God's help I had moved to a small cottage in the country with only one neighbor close by.

Shortly after that, I became the official recorder for the Centre and as such, attended all of the conferences and met many wonderful Christian people. My leisure time was spent walking alone through the fields or sitting quietly reading the first Bible I can remember owning.

Thinking back, I realize that just as quickly as I pleaded for his mercy, God held me in his arms. He kissed my forehead and wiped away my tears. He cleansed my body and my soul and gave me back my dignity. Over time, at my own pace, he taught me love.

Twenty years later, the game on television was over. My team had probably won but I wasn't paying attention. I turned off the set and sat quietly listening to the silence broken only by the sound of the wind, and watched the tranquil glow of the fire. As I thought of all of the wonderful things he had done for me I realized that, like the lepers, I had not thanked God for his many graces.

I praised God then for all that he had done and for the moments such as this of solitude and quiet repose, for the darkness that relaxed the eyes, the wood that nourished the fire which provided its warmth while, like a symphony from Chopin or Strauss, it danced in harmony with the wind and the twirling leaves. In this hectic and sometimes turbulent world that we have built, I silently thank him for the moments of peace and the love that he has created.

Death

Death to the person to whom it occurs is the end of life as we know it on this earth. Though the process of dying may be painful and/or frightening, all stops at death's arrival. However, to those who survive, it is only the beginning of the end. They now enter upon a time of healing, adjusting and continuing with life. Death is surely the most tragic of life's experiences. Yet, if one can go beyond the pain, the sorrow, the emptiness of seeing a loved one die, if one can detach oneself for a moment and see beyond that which is physically going on in front of them, then one would see that they are not witnessing a dramatic event but, rather, the fourth of four great miracles of life.

Death has been compared to a butterfly emerging from a cocoon, and it's a good comparison if we believe in God and the everafter. God has told us that he knew our name before our conception and that after death we are with him in eternity. Does this mean our human bodies are separate entities from what we are? Do we live within bodies that house us like a cocoon until we are ready to be released to fly on our own?

Is an electrician an electrician or a person who works as an electrician? If a person works as an electrician then that person is titled by only one aspect of their life, but aren't they so much more than that? As we are classed by one aspect of our lives like the color of our skin or the language we speak, the country we come from, and the way we dress, so are we recognized by our body without consideration for our souls. How often do we buy something because the packaging is pretty and inviting without actually giving careful consideration to what is inside the box? Do we see our loved ones in much the same way? We see their bodies, hear them talk and laugh, we hold them and hug them and are happy just to know they are there. When they die it's the end of their physical presence and this leaves us with great pain and emptiness. This, of course, is normal. Didn't Jesus cry when he heard of the death of John? Still, as Christians, we must know that our loved ones still live, only now they have been released of the burden of their bodies to live free and unhindered in eternal love.

On Thursday March 20 2003, I arrived on the sixth floor of the hospital and saw my sister, standing at the end of the hallway, leaning against the handrail, absently staring nowhere. She looked up as I approached and tried to smile, but it was a sad effort. We hugged and she began to cry. I waited, holding her tight until she regained her composure.

"What happened? How's mom?" I asked.

"It doesn't look good," My sister replied. "She called me this morning and said that she was in a lot of pain. When I arrived at the house she couldn't stand up, so I called an ambulance. The doctor is with her now."

We waited impatiently until the doctor exited the room and approached us. Over the years, she had not only been mom's physician, but also her friend and I noticed the gleam of a tear in her eye.

"I'm afraid it's not good news," She said. "Your mother's liver has stopped functioning. I'm sorry but there's nothing I can do for her. It's just a matter of time."

"How long do we have?", my sister asked in a broken voice.

"No one knows. It could be anytime, but usually no more than 36 hours. We can put her on life support to prolong the time, but nothing can be done to help her."

My sister looked at me before replying. "Mom made it clear that she didn't want to be kept on life support." I put my arm around her shoulder as she fought to maintain control. Then, with a sigh, my sister pleaded. "Please, just keep her comfortable so she won't suffer."

The doctor nodded and said we could go in to be with mom; then she left, looking forlorn as she walked down the long hallway. Mom was in a drug-induced coma when we entered. Standing by her bedside, I stared at her shrunken form – helpless, so unlike the strong woman I had known all of my life. Born in Montreal during the depression, she had spent her childhood in the troubled thirties and her adolescence in the war-torn years of the forties. During the last year of the war, mom worked in a munitions factory where she met a young man who, on October 27 1945, became her husband. As a young wife and mother, she was forced to leave Montreal for the first time in her life. My father had joined the navy and they moved to Nova Scotia where life was not easy for her since my father was often away at sea, and she spoke no English. However, by the end of the first year, she had taught herself the language and made friends to help pass the lonely time.

Then in 1980, disaster struck. Mom was diagnosed with lung cancer. With less than a 50 per cent chance of survival, she bravely prepared for the worst, and went under the knife as we waited and prayed. The surgery was successful and then, after 10 years of constant testing and treatment, she was declared a cancer survivor.

After her recovery, she volunteered many hours to help hospitalized patients, specializing in the comforting and consoling of other cancer victims. In 1997, she attended a volunteer's convention where she received honors for more than 1000 hours of service. Unfortunately, mom's health problems returned and soon she lost most of her mobility. Yet she continued to help by knitting booties for the hospital nursery (hundreds of newborn babies left the hospital wearing mom's booties) and by visiting patients whenever she could.

Now she lay in bed, weighing less than 100 pounds, completely helpless. We kissed her and stayed silently beside her for a while; then I left the room and went outside to call our brother. He was out of town and said that he would arrive as soon as possible. Returning to the room, I informed my sister. Without speaking, we knew that neither of us would be leaving mother's side until it was over.

The rest of the day, we alternated staying with mom or going outside to call friends and relatives. My brother arrived early that evening. We talked to mom, in case she could hear us, and tried to keep a brave face as we greeted those who came to visit. That night my sister slept by mother's side on a cot provided by the hospital, while my brother and I slept in the waiting room.

Roland R. J. Robert

On Friday March 21, mom's breathing was forced and shallow. She remained in a comatose state but we noticed that sometimes when we spoke to her while holding her hand, she would gently squeeze our fingers. Now we were sure she heard us – sometimes. Early in the afternoon, the hospital priest arrived and we said prayers while he administered last rights.

Saturday was her birthday, so at suppertime we got together with the visitors and, circling her bed, sang "Happy Birthday". My sister's husband brought a cake and we all had a piece while speaking of happy things to mom. Those who began to cry left the room in case she could hear them.

Later, we decided that my sister, brother, and I should each have 15 minutes alone with mom. When my turn came, I entered her room, closing the door behind me. I told mom that I loved her and thanked her for being such a good mother. We had always been very close.

Soon I became very peaceful. For a brief moment, I saw an image – almost like a thought – of a very handsome, neatly-bearded man leaning over mom and softly kissing her forehead. Then he was gone. Mom didn't move except to squeeze my hand ever so lightly. At the end of my 15 minutes, I left the room. Disturbed by my feelings, I went outside to be alone.

As I looked toward the stars, thoughts continued invading my mind: although we were surrounded by miracles that we no longer see, such as nature and the animals, we could divide life into four great miracles such as God himself for he is perfect love and the creator of all miracles. Then there is birth, for when a man and woman conceive a child, they bring into this world an eternal being, thus our body's only house the essence that is us, and which is made in God's likeness. The third might be life itself – from birth to childhood, adolescence to adulthood – all of the changes that take place in our lives, all of the things we see, do, and learn; these might all be part of one great miracle. Death is a sad thing because we know that we will no longer see the person that we love. We see it as the end. Yet, if we could separate ourselves from the sorrow and the grief, if we could go beyond the loneliness, the emptiness, the helplessness that we feel; then we might see that death is a miracle of transition into eternity. Therefore, although her body was leaving us, mom's essence would forever remain. If only I could get beyond my sorrow...

When I returned to her room, there was no visible change in her condition, but later that evening mom gave us a wonderful gift. To our delight, she opened her eyes for a few minutes. My brother, sister, and I made sure that we stood in her line of vision so that she could see that we were there. We smiled and told her how we loved her. That night the three of us slept in mom's room.

The next morning as I awoke, I saw a nurse standing quietly beside the bed, taking her pulse. As we got up, she looked at us with a sympathetic smile. Gathering by mom's side, we saw that her breathing was almost undetectable. We held her hands, told her we loved her and kissed her cheeks. One minute she was there. The next, she was gone. Her lifelong wish had been realized, for her children were with her in her last moments. It was Saturday March 22, 2003, 6:30 a.m. – her 76th birthday.

I didn't get past my grief that morning and it was with tear-filled eyes that I watched my mother pass away. Yet somewhere deep within my soul, a new strength was born that helped me through that traumatic time, and I knew that I had witnessed the last miracle of life.

Time has gone by since mom passed away. While she lived, I had often feared what would become of me when she was gone, yet now I realize that even in her last moments, Mom thought of her children. I don't go to her grave very often. I don't need to. Every day when I'm alone, I feel her presence and her warmth within my heart. Her wish was always for her children's happiness. Her love made it so.*

This piece was previously published in the Annals of St. Anne de Beaupré May 2005 issue Vol 119 – No 5, page 151.

Special Appreciation:

Louise Sproule, B.A. Psy., The Review
Laurie McClintock, B.A.
Carole Lafontaine, B.A. Psy.

www.ingramcontent.com/pod-product-compliance
Lightning Source LLC
Chambersburg PA
CBHW031324040426
42443CB00005B/205